Pathways to the
Waters of Grace

Pathways to the Waters of Grace

A Guide for a Church's Ministry with Parents Seeking Baptism for Their Children

David B. Batchelder

FOREWORD BY
Ronald P. Byars

WIPF & STOCK · Eugene, Oregon

PATHWAYS TO THE WATERS OF GRACE
A Guide for a Church's Ministry with Parents
Seeking Baptism for Their Children

Copyright © 2017 David B. Batchelder. All rights reserved. Except for brief quotations in critical publications or reviews, no part of this book may be reproduced in any manner without prior written permission from the publisher. Write: Permissions, Wipf and Stock Publishers, 199 W. 8th Ave., Suite 3, Eugene, OR 97401.

Wipf & Stock
An Imprint of Wipf and Stock Publishers
199 W. 8th Ave., Suite 3
Eugene, OR 97401

www.wipfandstock.com

PAPERBACK ISBN: 978-1-4982-8131-7
HARDCOVER ISBN: 978-1-4982-8133-1
EBOOK ISBN: 978-1-4982-8132-4

Manufactured in the U.S.A.

"Friend, guest or pilgrim" used by permission of Monastero di Bose, Italy.

"How to Be a Poet" copyright © 2005 by Wendell Berry, first published in *Given: New Poems*. Reprinted by permission of Counterpoint Press, Berkeley, California.

"Water," by Philip Larkin, reprinted by permission of Faber and Faber Limited, Essex, England.

Image of "Children on Tree" used with permission from Lyman Coleman.

Excerpt from *I Am Baptized*, by Richard Jespersen, used by permission of CSS Publishing Company, Lima, Ohio.

All Bible quotations taken from the New Revised Standard Version Bible, copyright © 1989, Division of Christian Education of the National Council of the Churches of Christ in the United States of America. Used by permission. All rights reserved.

In gratitude to West Plano Presbyterian Church (Plano, Texas), a baptized and baptizing community, whose love for sacramental liturgy and liturgical formation is evident in its commitment to the mission of Christ in the world.

Contents

Foreword by Ronald P. Byars | xi
Acknowledgments | xv
Introduction | xvii

Part 1: Shaping a New Vision

Chapter 1: Matters of Primary Concern | 3

Chapter 2: Conversion and Conversation | 11

Chapter 3: Setting the Space for Easter Conversation | 14
  1. Wonder Aloud and Often · 14
  2. Love Questions · 16
  3. Nurture the Imagination · 18
  4. Provide a Generous Hospitality · 22
  5. Treasure the Human Body · 24
  6. Cherish Symbols and Ritual · 27
  7. Pay Attention; Discern Readiness · 28
  8. Involve Others; Enlist and Nurture Sponsors · 31
  9. Make Connections; Bring It Home · 33
  10. Shape the Sunday Liturgy to Welcome All the Baptized · 36
  11. Reimagine All Christian Education as "Formation for Baptismal Living" · 38
  12. Live the Journey: Practice Baptismal Renewal and All Its Implications for the Church · 40

Summary · 41

CONTENTS

Part 2: Learning a New Practice

Introduction: A Contemplative-Reflective Model of
Sacramental Preparation | 45

Session 1: The Gift of a Child and the Journey of Faith | 51
    Opening Ritual · 51
    Personal Faith in Relationship to the Birth of a Child · 52
    Why Water? · 57
    Closing Ritual · 60

Session 2: Prayer and Baptismal Life | 63
    Opening Ritual · 63
    Prayer as Our Native Tongue · 63
    A Child's Capacity to Apprehend God and a
    Parent's Role as Fellow Learner · 68
    Practice at Home · 70
    Closing Ritual · 71

Session 3: Baptism as a Practiced Way of Life | 73
    Opening Ritual · 73
    Reflection on Experience · 73
    Water Stories and a Life of Conversion · 74
    Diving Deeper · 77
    Closing Ritual · 79

Session 4: Keeping Time in Baptismal Life | 80
    Opening Ritual · 80
    Calendars and Community · 80
    Creative Adaptation: Building Faith Traditions in the Home · 83
    Closing Ritual · 86

    Planting Seeds for Keeping Pentecost in the Home · 87
    Planting Seeds for Saint Nicholas Day, December 6 · 90

CONTENTS

Session 5: Baptismal Life as New Vocation | 92
    Opening Ritual · 92
    Keeping Time Revisited · 92
    Being "Called" in Baptism · 93
    Who Helped Shaped You? · 96
    Closing Ritual · 97

Session 6: Full Initiation—Water, Oil, Bread, and Wine | 98
    Opening Ritual · 98
    Baptismal Dignity and a Welcome to the Table · 98
    Wisdom and Beatitude: Formed in Worship · 103
    Living Our Baptismal Vows in the Liturgy:
    Faithful Formation of Children in Worship · 104
    The Shape of the Baptismal Rite · 107
    Closing Ritual · 109

Assessing Pastoral Challenges and Opportunities | 109

Appendix 1: Sponsors as Spiritual Companions | 123
Appendix 2: Enrichment Experience for Sponsors | 126
Bibliography | 133

Foreword

Baptism is one of those things that the church knows it has to do, even when it is not sure why. An old pattern of unwritten but powerful protocols is still in effect in many congregations. A child is born to members of the church (or, sometimes, alumni of the church), or perhaps it is a child whose only link to the church is through a grandparent or an acquaintance of the mother or father. A pastor is called and asked to save a date for a baptism on a day that has been determined to be convenient to family and friends. The pastor may or may not have a face-to-face conference with the parents to explain when the baptism will take place in the service, when they should come forward and where they will stand, what questions will be put to them, and what the answers must be, and may even spend a few moments with them trying to describe some of the layered meanings of baptism. Or, occasionally, a pastor may even agree to baptize at home, jeopardizing the ecclesial and communal significance of the sacrament.

Misconceptions abound and are not always challenged. Is the baptism intended to make sure that the child will be immune from any sort of peril in the next life? To introduce the child to family and friends? Is it a naming ceremony? A time of thanksgiving for the gift of new life? Or, does it engraft the baptized into the church, the body of Christ? Or is it an autonomous act preceding by a few years the opportunity for the baptized to "join the church"?

If there was ever a time when all parties concerned—families, pastors, and congregation—had a common understanding about this sacrament, such a time has passed. We have a sacrament whose meaning is likely to be defined by personal opinions formed with little exposure to the official teaching of the church, to which God has entrusted the sacraments. Should a conscientious pastor question the established protocols, she is likely to have a lot of explaining to do!

Of course, explaining is what pastors have been trained to do, never mind that explanations are likely to draw less respect than the excuse that "We have always done it this way." Nevertheless, more and more pastors have become emboldened by what one might call an ecumenical baptismal awakening in the past few decades. The churches have begun to recover the vision of the Christian life as a lifelong unfolding of our baptism. In this sacrament, we have been discovering how to discern the grace of God in Christ that embraces us before we are likely to have achieved any understanding of it, an act uniting us with all the baptized—living, dead, and yet to be born—in the body of Christ and the communion of saints, by the power of the Holy Spirit.

The bowl used for baptisms has been located and pulled off the shelf of the closet where it has been stored with the old Sunday school curriculum; the font the size of a large coffee cup has been replaced by one with room for an abundance of water; it has been moved into a position of prominence in the worship space, where it may be filled with water to be seen and even heard to remind us of our baptismal identity. Those leading worship may lead parts of the service from the font. Baptismal anniversaries may be noted and celebrated. So far, so good. But the old protocols are still powerful. How might we lead congregations to embrace with integrity a baptismal perspective of our life in Christ?

Integrity is the issue here, and integrity requires that actual practice be consistent with the teaching of the church. When the church's sacramental practice does not cohere with what the church believes and teaches, the teaching becomes irrelevant and the ritual itself becomes dysfunctional.

David Batchelder is pastor of the West Plano Presbyterian Church, a congregation of the Presbyterian Church (USA). The

FOREWORD

West Plano congregation has been led to center its life and mission around the sacraments, celebrating the Lord's Supper alongside the preaching of the Word every Sunday. As the congregation approaches the table to receive the bread and cup of the Holy Meal, they pass by the baptismal font filled with water. At West Plano they have learned to speak of ritual as "a way of thinking with the skin." In other words, they are absorbing the gospel of Jesus Christ in the sacramental rites as much as in words.

How do you prepare people to do that in a culture like ours, in which we are impatient until we get directly to the point, and want everything spelled out just so, in 140 characters or less if possible? Batchelder has taken advantage of the fact that there are teachable moments in people's lives when they are more disposed to risk spending some time in a period of discovery, open to something they may not have imagined themselves to be interested in before. One of those times is when they become parents, or learn that they will soon be parents, or are starting their lives together and looking ahead to the formation of a family.

In this helpful book, Batchelder describes the ways he has organized time with parents who are, in this particular moment, ready and even eager to think ahead about parenthood and how to guide the spiritual formation of their children, as well as clarify their own commitments. These are not classes, as such, because they are not designed primarily as vehicles for the transmission of information. The gatherings are marked by hospitality, flexibility, and attentiveness to the situations and experiences of the actual persons with whom he and other mentors are meeting. The goal of the gatherings is to help parents to deepen their own faith while also imagining how they, in their own households, might institute simple ways of exposing their children to the Christian faith in ways that draw upon and link to the communal practices of the church.

These gatherings are part of a larger congregational and ecclesial ecology, because the congregation is also learning how to support those who are bringing children for baptism or seeking it for themselves. The intention is that the congregation as a whole become a people who perceives and embraces an embodied gospel that not only takes the incarnation seriously, but encounters it in washing, eating, and drinking. It is an embodied gospel that is readily accessible to children—a gospel "caught" before it is "taught."

Of course, all of this takes time to implement, and to learn how to implement effectively. That opens another question, so important for ministry today, and that is, which of all the time-consuming pastoral possibilities takes priority? I suspect that the priorities that are most likely to go deepest and bear the most fruit over time are the ones that require just this sort of face-to-face, hospitable, flexible, patient, listening, and mentoring approach. I wish I had understood this better sooner.

Ronald P. Byars
Professor Emeritus of Preaching and Worship
Union Presbyterian Seminary

Acknowledgments

THIS BOOK WAS LIVED out in relationships before it took form in print. Those relationships have been vital to its completion. I wish to thank the following for their encouragement, help, and support: the Christian Initiation Study Group of the North American Academy of Liturgy, which graciously engaged me on Part 1 of the book; Sara Jo Mueller, who read my work with a keen eye for errors; Gláucia Vasconcelos Wilkey, friend and colleague, who offered critique and suggestions; my daughter Heidi Batchelder, who gave many helpful suggestions and brought professional scrutiny to footnotes and bibliography; Becki Williams, with whom I have practiced this ministry in the church I serve and whose suggestions proved invaluable (she also has graciously shared her own experience of this preparation process in Part 2, Session 7); and my wife, Nancy, whose patience and support encouraged me to complete a project so long in the making.

Introduction

THIS BOOK HAS BEEN writing itself for much of my professional life as a pastor. It has been "lived out" as much as "thought out." I imagine my readers as a communal gathering with a common concern for the future of the church. In the pages that follow, I invite readers into a theological reflection on the church's practice of baptism.

My hope is to articulate a theological vision for baptism and the ministry of nurture that surrounds it. More specifically, I want to help churches thoughtfully engage the kind of preparation we offer to parents who come seeking baptism for their children. Thus, the book is eminently practical. It sets forth an intentional ministry for how the church meets with its families before they arrive at the font and imagines a way of being for the church with parents who seek baptism for their children. At one time, many of us were such parents. If not parents ourselves, many of us were brought by parents, at a time beyond remembering, for Christian baptism. In that past, it is most likely that mothers and fathers received little by way of instruction beyond a theological explanation of baptism that might have included doctrinal statements concerning the sacrament. It most likely focused on practical matters such as when to come forward, where to stand, and what to say. If there was a time when such explanation was sufficient, it is surely now past. A soul-felt hunger has been stirring in many of us for something more hearty concerning baptism's meaning and the new life to which it births us. This

xvii

INTRODUCTION

book concerns itself with that meaning—not to be explained, but discovered experientially. The book affirms the blessing that children are gifts of God, including (for the purposes of this book) the marvelous way they rekindle in parents a new openness and wonder before the mystery of God in human experience. Such openness is fundamental to faith and essential to experience with God, who remains forever and always concerned with those who bear the divine image. That God seeks us out in love is what lies at the heart of every baptism. What is proposed here promises to deepen a parent's own joy and faithful discipleship. For this reason, the book asserts that a process of preparation has as much importance as the water-event of baptism itself.

This book is also offered as testimony. It bears witness to the author's personal blessing in rediscovering the sacramental tradition that lies at the heart of historic Reformed worship. Additionally, this book owes a debt of gratitude to the liturgical renewal movement among the historic churches. This movement has brought a rich sharing of insight and understanding for churches rediscovering baptism as the foundation for Christian unity and common purpose in mission. And then there is this: my life and ministry has been profoundly touched by this work of baptismal preparation. As with the churches I previously served, the one I now serve has deeply invested itself in this ministry. This book, therefore, bears witness to what has taken flesh in local worshiping communities, where Scripture, water, oil, bread, and wine reside at the center of our common life. The most practical sections of this book have been thoroughly tested with many groups of parents, and this offering has evolved organically through years of practice and reflection on experience.

In Part 1, I set forth specific emphases that characterize this prebaptismal preparation process. These are not principles, but matters of primary concern practiced throughout the process. When given due attention, this process creates an environment of holy expectation that opens space for deep personal experience. To this end, the process proposed in this book has to do not only with *what* is done by way of preparation, but *how* it is done. Content should not be separated from context, and everything communicates something of significance. Therefore, we attend to that "something" with intentionality.

In Part 2, I describe six formational sessions. They ought not to be thought of as classes, because there is no curriculum. Rather, what is presented is a guide that suggests reflection, conversation, understanding, insight, wonder, and prayer. My aim is to present enough detail so that any leader can take up these suggestions and incorporate them in ministry.

In the late 1970s, Alexander Schmemann attributed contemporary spiritual atrophy to the fact that baptism is "*absent* from our life," "the Church's liturgy," and "our piety," "and has so lost its power to shape our worldview, i.e. our basic attitudes, motivations, and decisions."[1] He believed that the recovery of faithful baptismal practice was "the source and the starting point of all liturgical renewal and revival" and "that the church reveals her own nature to herself, constantly renews herself as a community of the baptized."[2] My hope is that this book's proposal for prebaptismal preparation of parents will help us step in this direction.

---

1. Schmemann, *Of Water and the Spirit*, 8–9.
2. Ibid., 38.

Part 1:
Shaping a New Vision

Chapter 1:
Matters of Primary Concern

COMING TO TERMS, PERSONALLY, with God's claim in baptism has remained foremost in my own flesh and bone because of shared parenting experience with my wife, Nancy. The births of two wonderful children within a few short years of one another set us on an uncharted journey of discovering how faith might root most meaningfully within our home. In those days, we quickly came to understand the many ways our children revealed the mystery of God-with-us. Seven years later we were surprised to discover that we would be parents again, this time with twin sons. This offered a rare opportunity for our older children, in the months leading up to the twin's birth, to partner with us in preparing both our home and our lives for two more Batchelders. Together as a family of six, we wondered about the mystery of God underway in the transformation of our family.

The late Roman Catholic lay theologian Mark Searle spoke of the birth of a child as a "word-of-God-event."[1] We took this wisdom to heart. As parents, we endeavored to tune our lives to that word of God and its meaning for us as a small community of the baptized. In the time that has passed, we have continued to orient our family life according to this unexpected "word" with its surprising disclosures. Years of reflection have situated me firmly in a baptismal ecclesiology that affirms baptism as *event and process*. I am compelled to remain at water's edge. I am wet still. By

---

1. "Infant Baptism Reconsidered," in Searle, *Vision*, 163.

grace, we are washed, reborn, buried and raised, newly clothed, and incorporated into Christ's church through baptism. In its Sunday gatherings, the church itself is reconstituted as Christ's body sent into the world to serve. Thus, Christian baptism is both gift and call to a new way of being that entails lifelong conversion to all God intends for us.

Contemporary Christianity suffers from an inherited preoccupation with the punctiliar moment of baptism, that is, with the application of water and the spoken name of the triune God. Inadequate and insufficient preparation for baptism (or, often, none at all) has contributed to theological distortions that leave baptism stripped of its meaning and mystery. It is no wonder that baptism has been vulnerable to sentimental cultural projections that trivialize the sacrament, a problem compounded by minimalistic liturgical practice. Fonts no larger than birdbaths containing little water are unable to carry the weighty meaning of baptismal dying and rising. Also overlooked is the relationship of the *before-and-after* to that water-event. While both ministries are formational, one cultivates a readiness to make baptismal vows while the other thoughtfully engages living a baptismal identity in all our social and ecclesial engagements. What happens before and after baptism is no less important than the actual baptismal water-event itself. The primary focus in this volume, however, is given to what comes prior to baptism. It takes seriously the church's formational ministry with parents who come seeking the baptism of their child, conceiving such ministry more in terms of faith formation than instruction.

We are living in the midst of a significant and momentous transition from an educational orientation grounded in the growth of knowledge, to an orientation grounded in changed patterns of living that fully integrate thinking, feeling, and doing. Most commonly this is spoken of as *formation*. A church committed to shifting from an educational to a formational mindset and practice will most likely encounter difficulty and resistance because Christians, particularly Protestants, are deeply invested in religious knowledge as a central attribute of strong faith. Churches commonly lament

CHAPTER 1: MATTERS OF PRIMARY CONCERN

rising biblical illiteracy, declining church school attendance, and the fusion of cultural mythologies (often originating in the Magic Kingdom of Disney[2]) with biblical stories.

Fundamentally, faith formation attends to the deepest-seated desires of the human heart, since "our ultimate love is constitutive of our identity," writes James K. A. Smith. He continues, "It's not what I think that shapes my life from the bottom up; it's what I desire, what I love, that animates my passion."[3] Smith elaborates:

> It's not so much that we're intellectually convinced and then we muster the willpower to pursue what we ought; rather, at a precognitive level, we are attracted to a vision of the good life that has been painted for us in stories and myths, images and icons. It is not primarily our minds that are captivated but rather our imaginations that are captured, and when our imagination is hooked, we're hooked.[4]

These insights have given rise to new metaphors with which to reimagine the nurture of the baptized. "Apprenticeship"[5] helps to capture the comprehensiveness of a formational vision of ministry because it encompasses understanding but sets it in the context of ethical, moral, and spiritual competency. Such a shift in thinking is moving Protestant churches to reconnect with the language of *catechesis* as a helpful broadening, deepening, and expanding of the more common language of education. Debra Dean Murphy speaks of Christian catechesis as "a practice, or set of practices, informed at the heart by doxology."[6] Central to catechesis, therefore, is experience in the sacramental liturgy of the church and the ebb and flow of our lives as we are gathered and sent each Lord's Day. Christian formation, therefore, is rooted in the doxological life of

---

2. For further study regarding cultural mythologies see Budde, *(Magic) Kingdom of God*; Smith, *Desiring the Kingdom*; Miller, *Consuming Religion*.

3. Smith, *Desiring the Kingdom*, 51.

4. Ibid., 54.

5. *General Directory for Catechesis*, 60. See #67, where "apprenticeship" is central to an understanding of formation as distinct from education.

6. Murphy, *Teaching That Transforms*, 11.

the faith community. It is necessarily comprehensive in its efforts to address living baptismal life as one of ongoing conversion in faith practices and the cultivation of God-inspired desires.

It is possible to think that this shift from education to formation is a new development belonging to this millennium. In fact, formational ministry leading to baptism has ancient roots in the catechumenate developed during the first five centuries of Christianity. Indeed, contemporary Christianity is marked, in part, by attempts to reappropriate the ancient model of the catechumenate[7] and adapt it for present ministry. For example, following Vatican II, the Roman Catholic Church implemented this model in the *Rite of Christian Initiation of Adults (RCIA)*. Now many Protestant denominations have begun to adapt a model of the catechumenate and the pastoral/liturgical wisdom that takes form in a process of faith development, marked by ritual stages, leading to baptism and full initiation. There is much to be gained in taking this wisdom to heart by undertaking a process of prebaptismal preparation that is patterned, public, communal, formational, and makes use of symbols and ritual.

In truth, many denominations expect something to take place prior to baptism. For example, the Presbyterian Church (USA), in its "Directory for Worship," assigns responsibility for baptismal preparation to each church's session, which also authorizes the celebration of the sacrament. The session is to admit to baptism "children of believers, after appropriate instruction and discussion with the parent(s) or one(s) rightly exercising parental responsibility, acquainting them with the significance of what God is doing in this act, and with the special responsibilities on parents and congregations for nurturing the baptized person in the Christian life."[8] Surely it is prudent to ask: What, exactly, might this all look like in practice? What shape should it take? How might such "instruction

---

7. The catechumenate is the process in which the church welcomes new members into its community and is based on ancient patterns of formation rooted in the early church. The word "catechumenate" means "to hear," or more literally, "to echo in the ear."

8. PC(USA), *Book of Order*, W-2.3012b.

CHAPTER 1: MATTERS OF PRIMARY CONCERN

and discussion" be helpfully offered to parents who contemplate taking vows for their child's baptism?

A similar call for thoughtful baptismal preparation is found in the Evangelical Lutheran Church in America's (ELCA) document *The Use of the Means of Grace*. Under the heading "Baptism includes instruction and nurture in the faith for a life of discipleship," Principle 19 states:

> When infants and young children are baptized, the parents and sponsors receive instruction and the children are taught throughout their development. . . . The parish education of the congregation is part of baptismal ministry. Indeed, all of the baptized require life-long learning, the daily re-appropriation of the wonderful gifts given in Baptism.[9]

What I have found missing in denominational statements is any conception of what such instruction might look like. Without appropriate patterns of ministry, church leaders have employed the transfer-of-information model that views faith as an agreed upon set of beliefs. Much more helpful is to take the liturgical rite of baptism itself and allow it to spark the imagination and plant seeds for in-depth conversation about the grace of God in human experience. For instance, in the Presbyterian *Book of Common Worship*, parents are asked, "Relying on God's grace, do you promise to live the Christian faith and teach that faith to your child?"[10] Lutherans using the *Evangelical Lutheran Worship* ask, "As you bring *your children* to receive the gift of baptism, you are entrusted with responsibilities: . . . Do you promise to help *your children* grow in the Christian faith and life?"[11] It is good and profitable to ask what it might mean for parents to live the Christian faith with the intent of nurturing faith and how this challenge is affected by single parenthood or divorced or blended families.

Many baptismal rites include renunciations, e.g., "Do you renounce the ways of sin that draw you from the love of God?"

---

9. ELCA, *Use of the Means of Grace*, 25.
10. PC(USA), *Book of Common Worship*, 406.
11. ELCA, *Evangelical Lutheran Worship*, 584.

Churches have some obligation in forming parents to live into the meaning of this promise. Similarly, parents are asked to teach the faith to their children. Churches are responsible to explore what this looks like, helping to shape families in practices that live out the promise. Each family context brings a special set of questions that bear consideration. It makes sense, therefore, that a handbook approach to prebaptismal preparation will miss the mark. Instead, the church is wiser to share its life and wisdom in a process of formation that discerns with parents what shape baptismal faith might have in each family's home. Much can be gained by hearing the questions that the baptismal rite implicitly asks and allowing these questions to probe minds, hearts, and imaginations in a communal encounter with the mystery of God's grace in the sacraments.

Faith does not exist as a set of ideas to be exchanged, but as a way of being in the flesh. Faith is far more verb than noun. We might even speak of faith-ing. For faith has no presence except as we live it out in the presence of others. Though we talk of faith and what it looks like, faith does not make its appearance in our words. Only in the manner of our living is faith most truly what it is—the salvation of God in us and the world. We must never mistake faith for doctrine, as important as doctrine is, because the substance of faith exists or does not exist in the virtues, ethics, and character of our human engagements. This preparation for baptism process expresses such faith even as it purposefully forms lives more deeply in the mystery of *God-with-us*, *Christ-through-us*, and the *Spirit-in-us*. Only such an understanding of faith as this can make sense of Saint Francis's famous injunction to preach the gospel and, if necessary, use words.

This book sets forth a particular kind of coming together for parents, sponsors, and the church's spiritual guides, who are referred to in some traditions as catechists and mystagogues. Together, they share an experience of deep mystery: the contemplation of a God who, through Jesus Christ and in the power of the Spirit, takes us into God's own life through baptism.

CHAPTER 1: MATTERS OF PRIMARY CONCERN

The goal of this book is not to encourage imitation but rather adaptation. Each local setting calls for its own contextualization of the process. What is proposed in this work has nothing in common with the various formulas for spiritual success that make frequent appearance on religious bestsellers lists. Eschewing quantifiable measures of success, this process of baptismal preparation seeks to be an authentic gospel witness to the grace that claims us and turns us outward in service to neighbor and stranger. The sessions suggested here are about inquiry, disclosure, recognition, and response whereby participants come into a greater fullness of a life graced by the presence of God. Each local community, therefore, is encouraged to take into its own corporate flesh a pattern of ministry that leads to and flows from the water of new birth.

This proposal of intentional preparation for baptism is not a program. It is a way of being church that is not scripted ahead of time. Its form is grounded in a fundamental pattern that honors particular values and virtues that ought not only be considered seriously, but ought to be embodied in each communal encounter with parents. Over time, the repeated practice of this process will bring leaders to insights and learning that can be woven into each new cycle of preparation. Such reflection on the church's experience of this ministry is a critical responsibility and privilege of leaders, because with the application of new insight, the church can grow more competent and skillful in being a community of strong baptismal identity.

It helps immensely to think of this practice as an intentioned conformity to a patterned way of being before God and others that leads to an embodied rather than theoretical knowledge. Such knowledge is learned only in the doing, for the very nature of what can be known is inaccessible to speculative thought. Indeed, the mystery and marvel of baptismal grace is that it is less taught than caught. It is grasped from the inside out rather than the outside in. And then, as always, is the pondering of its meaning. Reflection on practice is essential. William Sloane Coffin Jr. captured centuries of ancient wisdom when he wrote, "Never have an experience and miss the meaning."[12] The conviction of this writer is that what we do in our flesh forms and informs the whole person—thought, desires, affections, behavior, and allegiances.

---

12. Coffin, *Letters to a Young Doubter*, 27.

Chapter 2:
Conversation and Conversion

I HAVE LONG BEEN intrigued by Luke's Gospel narrative of the encounter of the two disciples with the risen Christ on the road to Emmaus (24:13–35). It is one of Scripture's most compelling stories of transition and conversation leading to a spiritual awakening; a seemingly accidental conversation blossoms into meal fellowship bursting with new life. Christ-the-stranger is revealed to his companions as Christ-the-host, making them tablemates together. Ever since, the Emmaus road has served as a metaphor for the life to which the baptized are called, one experienced richly in the sacramental life of the church.

As the baptized and baptizing community, we are people of the way. We find our path as we engage, conversationally, the mystery of God in the crucified and risen Christ. We do not walk this way alone, but with each other and Christ in our midst. It is a journey from grace to grace. In the Luke text, divine disclosure begins in *conversation* leading to *conversion*. These words, conversation and conversion, have a close relation with one another. Conversion begins in conversation. As the Emmaus story reveals, a change of heart, mind, or behavior has its beginnings in the flow of particular social interactions that entice us, stir us, provoke us, inform us, correct us, and challenge us. We discover, usually in retrospect, that our hearts have been sparked with a newness given us by the grace of God. The converting possibility of conversation cannot be controlled or predicted; it must be trusted. Though we cannot often trace specific conversations to transforming experience, such conversations help bring us to a new willingness to see, feel, think, and act differently than before.

Preparation for baptism is fundamentally conversational. Its habitat is the mutual sharing of life and faith with all the hopes and fears we carry. While church leaders are eager to share wisdom and theological insight with participating parents, it is not helpful to present it as "material to be covered." For what begins as a promising conversation of mutual sharing becomes sabotaged when well-meaning leaders succumb to anxiousness about getting everything in before time runs out. Looming large is the temptation to manage the conversation so as to ensure some particular theological content gets addressed. Under such pressure, it is hard for leaders to attend the sacred exchange as it unfolds.

Consider the alternative of an approach that is more temperate in its pace—something akin to a Sabbath rest. In such a reimagined process, the conversational manner of being together is recognized and nurtured as an essential witness to baptismal identity. Moreover, this approach helps make possible a form of listening that is discerning of the experience in its entirety and where nothing is really "off topic" despite how it first might appear. Skillful leaders will notice and consider all that unfolds, even if no immediate response to some particular matter presents itself in the moment.

What counts is being fully present to one another because in such openness, "God happens," says Rowan Williams.[1] The kind of conversation being imagined here, like water itself, will find its own course especially when something of deep feeling is stirred, as is often the case. Indeed, such stirring is to be hoped for since the mystery of baptism is about living the meaning of the crucified and risen Christ exactly where we each find ourselves in our daily lives. Leadership is responsible for cultivating a conversation-friendly environment that is always open to the unexpected. Such openness informs the pattern of each shared encounter offered in this book.

---

1. Williams, *Where God Happens*, 24.

CHAPTER 2: CONVERSATION AND CONVERSION

It may help to think of conversation in these terms: conversation is a skill, an artful way of being in relation to others that is hospitable, dignifying, and loving. Unlike "telling," a conversational mode of being makes space for others to be genuinely themselves without threat of judgment. In providing such space for others, the body of Christ behaves true to its self. Such a corporate "self" as the church is called to be is strongly countercultural in several ways. The culture is saturated with a vociferous and combative media that schools the public in all manners of verbal tactics aimed to win arguments, silence the opposition, and hijack conversation to serve personal agendas. Let us instead imagine such conversations in the light of the Emmaus story. I suggest we claim this dialogue as *Easter conversation*, as an essential spiritual practice through which members of Christ's body contemplate together the grace of God at work in our lives.

To be considered next are matters of special attention that underlie the practice of this preparation process. These are attributes, virtues, or values that serve to maintain the integrity of the process as it unfolds. When given careful attention, a sense of holy expectation can grow within each participant, helping them to be more fully present to the mystery of grace. What follows pertains to the character of this process—*how* it is led and shared. *What* is done in particular gatherings will be addressed afterward.

Chapter 3:
Setting the Space for Easter Conversation

1. Wonder Aloud and Often

IN A WIKIPEDIA WORLD, we do less and less wondering about things; we look them up instead. The mind's more natural mode is one of reasoning that deliberates cause and effect, analyzes reality, and tests plausibility. In this sense, reasoning tends to zero in on the subject at hand. Wondering opens itself up as wide as possible to the fullness of the reality being experienced. It adopts a mode of perceiving and pondering that is not driven by any specific hoped for outcome. Instead, wondering accepts what comes to awareness and takes delight in it with an innocent curiosity.

Because wondering does not have a predetermined point of arrival, it is characterized as readiness to be met by something unforeseen. We experience a thought, insight, or new perspective coming to our awareness that we did not have before in quite the way we find we are now thinking about it. Wondering needs time, space, the absence of distraction, and encouragement. The encouragement we need comes in the form of validation. Wondering is not idle indulging, but is a form thoughtfulness possessing great value.

Wondering positions us to see truths that might have gone unnoticed *in* our lives and *about* our lives before God. For example, a very basic but essential question to be asked in a group

CHAPTER 3: SETTING THE SPACE FOR EASTER CONVERSATION

preparing for baptism is, "How did I get here? . . . to this preparation for baptism process? . . . in this church? . . . at this time in my life?" Such a question may lead in many directions because it is intends to help people consider how their participation in this prebaptismal process might not be solely due to personal decision-making. Wondering questions like these presume that our lives are not manufactured merely by the exercise of individual volition. Making this kind of inquiry leaves us open to the movement of a personal God, acting graciously towards the creation God loves. Entertaining such questions as these brings us face to face with mystery and the possibility of God's unseen ways calling, leading, and stirring in us a desire previously unnamed. Wondering questions orient the conversation towards faith and invite us to trust a God who is for us rather than against us.

Such wonder as I am describing is the basis for all theological reflection. We reflect out of our personal lived experience, rather than in the abstract. This experience is usually a mixed bag of joys and sorrows, elation and heartbreak, achievement and failure. A living faith seeks to be in continual dialogue with all experience. Only in this way are we able to come to terms with who we are as those God calls by grace and commissions to serve. Making baptismal vows that promise over time to "live the Christian faith and teach that faith to our children" surely looks to engage our thinking concerning the presence of God in all of life's experiences.

Wondering, then, is a spiritual discipline through which we remain attentive to a truth that is much larger than first meets the eye. In fact, this truth cannot be exhausted. Yet, this does not cause distress because to wonder is to be drawn near the Holy One, the divine presence itself. Although wonderment does not resolve all questions (even giving rise to new ones not previously considered), wonderment nonetheless feeds the soul with a sense of contentment that our lives are tended by a God who will never let us go.

Applied in the process of baptismal preparation, wondering asks that leaders be sensitive to pace the conversation with care not to make transitions too quickly, before all are ready to do so. Some will find their words only after listening to others, when it might seem the subject has been addressed. Among leaders, therefore, patience is necessary, for it is in the silences that some fresh insight gestates before it is shared. When we lead parents in wonder, we invite them to holy ground and communion with God.

2. Love Questions

In the summer of 1903, German poet Rainier Maria Rilke wrote a series of letters to a young poet. In one of them he said:

> You are so young, so much before all beginning, and I would like to beg you, dear Sir, as well as I can, to have patience with everything unresolved in your heart and to try to love the questions themselves as if they were locked rooms or books written in a very foreign language. Don't search for the answers, which could not be given to you now, because you would not be able to live them. And the point is, to live everything. Live the questions now. Perhaps then, someday far in the future, you will gradually, without even noticing it, live your way into the answer.[1]

Rilke's words have been embraced by a growing segment in Christianity that has become tired of religious absolutism and weary of claims to theological certainty. This segment also finds a new at-homeness with mystery and its relationship to material forms in sacramental worship. Faith is not the acquisition of answers, but trust in the midst of not having it all figured out. This increasing comfort with mystery does not diminish the mind or the search for truth. It is a more honest and humble seeking that freely admits to doubt, confusion, and uncertainty.

We are, all of us, doubters. The freedom to question bears witness to faith's invitation to "come and see," a favorite motif of John's Gospel. We do not arrive as people of faith. We live in the tension of knowing only in part. When parents come to the church seeking baptism for their children, it is likely (if their faith is church-bred) that they have come to conceive of faith as a belief system. Vestiges

---

1. Rilke, *Letters to a Young Poet*, 34–35.

CHAPTER 3: SETTING THE SPACE FOR EASTER CONVERSATION

of such thinking continue to do harm whenever people worry whether they are "correctly" believing in God. Indeed, there is still much Christianity advocating itself as a set of correct theological precepts. The preparation process presented here radically departs from this approach.

This process provides and protects a safe space for seekers wanting to make sense of their place in God's world. To be sure, such seeking necessarily calls the church to open for exploration its theological treasure trove, but not as a dogmatic dispensing of truth claims. The church's convictions about meaning are shared with humility and a respect for what cannot be known. What the church believes about baptism and the life born from the water will be offered in the form of invitation and witness. As invitation, participants are welcome to explore, question, challenge, and even disagree as they try on for themselves the heritage of meaning that the church has preserved through the generations. As witnesses, leaders will share the testimony of God's grace from their own personal lives as well as from the church's liturgy, where the fullest expression of baptism's sacramental meaning comes to flower in the Sunday assembly.

The love of questions befits baptismal life with much of Christianity still preoccupied with cultivating certainty. Baptism begins a life of ongoing conversion. It does not complete it. Our questions help us live out with others a newness of life born in the waters of the font. However long it has been since our new birth in the font, we all continue as works in progress. No human being is alone with her or his questions. As with prayer, our questions also belong to the faith community to be shared, loved, and lived. Such a corporate way of being present before God in community is one aspect of what it means to "walk wet." Our openness before God and willingness to trust dries up when we feel compelled to affirm certainties that leave no room for questions. Just as the potter cannot form the bowl if the clay has become dry, so living out our questions together helps us stay wet. One of the great mystagogues of the fourth century, Theodore of Mopsuestia (c. 350–428), told the newly baptized, "You are born in water because you were formed originally from earth and water; . . . This is what a potter does when a vase he is shaping from clay becomes spoilt: he shapes it again in water and so it recovers its true form."[2] The following prayer gives voice to the truth of our ongoing formation:

> Merciful God,
>
> as a potter fashions a vessel from humble clay,
>
> you form us into a new creation.
>
> Shape us, day by day,
>
> through the cross of Christ your Son,
>
> until we pray as continually as we breathe
>
> and all our acts are prayer;
>
> through Jesus Christ
>
> and in the mystery of the Holy Spirit, we pray. **Amen.**[3]

3. Nurture the Imagination

Many years ago, I visited Pittsburgh's Carnegie Museum of Art to see a wonderful exhibit of black-and-white photographs by W. Eugene Smith. He was one of America's greatest photographers of the twentieth century. All 193 exhibit photographs were taken of Pittsburgh during 1955. Information provided at the exhibit informed viewers that Smith was attracted to signs that spoke to fundamental human ideals. One section of the exhibit was devoted to photographs of street signs artfully juxtaposed with people and buildings. The names were striking. There was "Mercy Street," "Friendship Avenue," "Pride Street," "Loyalty Way," and "Progress Street." What caught my attention was a photograph of an old sedan sitting parked all alone along the side of a wooded road, save for a mailbox and a street sign that said "Dream." After some investigative work, I learned that "Dream Street" was no longer on the map in Pittsburgh. At one time it ran for several blocks in

---

2. Yarnold, *Awe-Inspiring Rites of Initiation*, 187–88.
3. PC(USA), *Book of Common Worship*, 108.

CHAPTER 3: SETTING THE SPACE FOR EASTER CONVERSATION

the vicinity of Pittsburgh's West Liberty Avenue. Today, that same area is overgrown with vegetation with the opening barely visible. We might wonder ourselves what has become of faith's capacity to dream.

To dream is to think with full powers of the imagination. Without the imagination, we will not be able to live God's promised future in the present. It is tragic, then, that our imaginations suffer atrophy as we move out of childhood and grow older. The gift of a child presents each parent with an opportunity to see the world anew with awe and marvel. Madeleine L'Engle calls attention to children's capacity for creativity and its importance to faith. "Creativity opens us to revelation."[4]

One great gift of God offered adults in children is that of rekindling our diminishing imaginations. The food of the imagination consists of metaphor, poetry, story, color, sound, silence, image, and the tactile. All these belong to baptismal preparation. Words should be thoughtfully chosen before being spoken, read, prayed, and sung in this process. But words alone are not capable of disclosing the fullness of meaning to which our Easter conversations about baptism aspire. According to Mark Searle, the reason why the imagination is so essential to faith is because the imagination "is not what we see or think: it is rather the lens through which we see, the very patterns within which we think."[5]

Given by God to the church, the sacraments are more poem than prose in the way they mediate their meaning. Because poetry is so expansive, it can be very frustrating for those who want to pin down truth. Poetry opens up rather than narrows down. Poetry often takes opposites and affirms them both! Poetry feasts on metaphors that are so roomy we can't be sure we will ever understand all they intend to say. So there's always excess, a superabundance of meaning that keeps truth-seekers coming back again and again for new insights awaiting disclosure. It is true of both the language of poetry and baptismal meaning that they cannot be understood through mere explanation. They seek to inhabit the imagination.

4. L'Engle, *Walking on Water*, 80.
5. "Images and Worship," in Searle, *Visions*, 127.

Only then will we perceive God's truth, or better yet, be apprehended by it. As with poetry, so it is with the grace of baptism and the Lord's Supper, which speak truth to our imaginations in metaphors. As we soak in sacramental imagery, we allow baptism to work its power reshaping how we see the world, and how we act in the world making us God's collaborators in the transformation of the world.

Some years ago, poet Martin Espada, considered by some the Pablo Neruda[6] of North America, gave the commencement address at Hampshire College. He said, "No change for the good ever happens without being imagined first."[7] There was a time in early Western Christianity when this truth was more readily grasped than it is today. At that time, the church practiced a form of imaginative reflection on sacramental experience called "mystagogy." The word itself sounds alien to those who have not heard it, however, it would be wise for us to recover it in our vocabulary. The value of the word "mystagogy" lies in the practice to which it points, a practice that fully engages the imaginative powers given us by God. William Harmless describes mystagogy as "less an explanation and more an exploration; it is less an explication and more an evocation. It works like diving gear: it allows one to breathe in depths otherwise inaccessible and to swim down and surface buried treasures otherwise overlooked."[8]

Because of their particular skills in facilitating this kind of reflection, those who nurtured young Christians in baptismal living were sometimes called "mystagogues." As we look for those who might have skills and ability to lead such a way of reflection in this ministry, we might consider the wisdom of poets among us, who already know to treasure images and metaphors as well as the silences between them. Giving poetry a place in this preparation process can help loosen our minds from the hyperliteralism that grips so much of religion. The poet Wendell Berry offers wise

---

6. Considered by many as one of the greatest poets of the twentieth century, and winner of the 1971 Nobel Prize in literature.

7. Espada, "Republic of Poetry."

8. Harmless, *Augustine and the Catechumenate*, 365–67.

CHAPTER 3: SETTING THE SPACE FOR EASTER CONVERSATION

counsel for those called to lead parents in their exploration of Christian baptism.

> Make a place to sit down.
> Sit down. Be quiet.
> You must depend upon
> affection, reading, knowledge,
> skill—more of each
> than you have—inspiration,
> work, growing older, patience,
> for patience joins time
> to eternity. Any readers
> who like your work,
> doubt their judgment.
>
> Breathe with unconditional breath
> the unconditional air.
> Shun electric wire.
> Communicate slowly. Live
> a three-dimensioned life;
> stay away from screen.
> Stay away from anything
> that obscures the place it is in.
> There are no unsacred places;
> there are only sacred places
> and desecrated places.
>
> Accept what comes from silence.
> Make the best you can of it.
> Of the little worlds that come
> out of the silence, like prayer
> prayed back to the one who prays,
> make a poem that does not disturb
> the silence from which it came.[9]

9. Berry, "How to Be a Poet." Leaders might contemplate this poem as guidance on how to be a mystagogue.

PART 1: SHAPING A NEW VISION

4. Provide a Generous Hospitality

Hospitality is essential in all its dimensions to this process. The room design and space should be hospitable in terms of seating, air temperature, furnishings, and the keeping of visual and audible distractions to a minimum. Hospitality ought to include food and drink appropriate to the time of day. What is offered should communicate to participants that the church has given thought to what is nutritious, delightful to the taste, and appealing to the eye, all with just a touch of extravagance. As with many religions, Christianity extends hospitality with food. Surely there are a few in every church who have a keen sensitivity to such matters of hospitality. Their gifts should be welcomed into the preparation process so long as they do not also bring an obsessive anxiousness that everything must be "perfect." The church is not about perfection, but the power of grace to take what we offer and make it more than sufficient for the occasion. Let it be remembered that anxiousness adds tension to the room and clouds the atmosphere that hospitality seeks to create. And remember that what is being prepared for is an Easter conversation that requires needed space that welcomes and encourages reflection.

Hospitality includes all matters pertaining to the leadership of this process, including how participants are welcomed, the use of prepared materials, the guidance given to the conversation, care for those who speak often as well as those who defer to others, and everyone's comfort with silence. In this regard, we see that hospitality has much to do with the embodied presence of the leaders themselves. This is especially important because we want to encourage within all participants an openness to share questions, doubts, and hopes. We want to help alleviate any anxiety that what one might say aloud is wrong. Many parents, perhaps most, feel apprehensive that they lack the necessary competence to teach their child the faith. Hospitality helps to relax these emotions in an atmosphere of refreshing graciousness. To this point, Mark Searle offers wise counsel. He writes that we do not so much promise to teach our children merely what we know as much as we promise to

CHAPTER 3: SETTING THE SPACE FOR EASTER CONVERSATION

learn again anew the story with them. "It is chiefly by [our] living the Christian story," he writes, "that [our] children will come to pick it up and to develop the skills necessary to be faithful to it."[10] At a very basic level, this preparation process is Christ's invitation to "come and see" all over again. Parents are co-learners with their children who together commit to live the Christian story as if they are newly born to it—which they are, as are we all. The important matter of hospitality will be revisited in Part 2 of this book in relation to the specific sessions themselves. For now, we might consider the remarkable witness of the Monastery of Bose, situated halfway between Milan and Turin near the foothills of the Italian Alps. It began in the mid 1960s and developed as an ecumenical community renowned for its hospitality, receiving thousands of visitors annually. On its website is the following invitation. Its generosity of spirit is inspiring.

> Friend, Guest or Pilgrim: You may come to Bose for any number of reasons: to seek a quiet place to rest a while, a hill where you can pray, brothers and sisters with whom to discover a life in communion, a place to listen to God's Word, a place of silence. . . . The community asks nothing of you, but invites you to listen, transform your worries into concern for others, and seek peace. Here you have the opportunity to reflect on your life, to take part in the community's prayer and praise of God, and to listen to the One who has led you to this secluded place, this silent spiritual desert, to speak to your heart. You also have the chance to talk with others about your church and social commitments. During the community's work hours, you may find that you feel alone: these times are opportunities to meet Christ in peace and silence.[11]

---

10. Searle, "Infant Baptism Reconsidered," 48–49.
11. Monastero di Bose, "Friend, guest or pilgrim," http://www.monasterodibose.it/en/hospitality.

PART 1: SHAPING A NEW VISION

5. Treasure the Human Body

It might already be apparent that "matter" matters. This is especially true of the human body and in a faith where incarnation is central. What has been said concerning hospitality is not merely a strategy to gain access to the human spirit. The new creation we become in Christ through baptism is nothing at all if it does not include all our fleshly existence with bone and blood, muscle and sinew. Hospitality is just one important practice by which the church is its true self in the skin of its members. Because the sacraments—baptism and the Lord's Supper—are so substantially earthly, preparation for sacramental participation itself closely attends to the materiality of our faith.

From its very beginning, Christianity has wrestled with the scandal of the incarnation and all it affirms about God's creation. God did not make us as brains on stilts, but as embodied beings. The Word became flesh, not disembodied intelligence. This is why our faith is expressed in washing bodies, anointing heads, eating bread, and drinking wine. Our body life is second to nothing in coming before the God whose masterpiece we are.

Nathan Mitchell writes that "our fear of putting God and body together in the same sentence has created all kinds of mischief in Christian theology. It has led us to construct a kind of cognitive apartheid which exalts spirit over body, mind over matter, thought over action."[12] Coming to terms with the nature of humanity as body and soul, Tertullian (d. 225) writes that "the flesh is the very condition on which salvation hinges."[13] Drawing upon the ritual of baptism, Tertullian continues:

> The flesh, indeed, is washed, in order that the soul may be cleansed; the flesh is anointed, that the soul may be consecrated; the flesh is signed (with the cross), that the soul too may be fortified; the flesh is shadowed with the imposition of hands, that the soul also may be illuminated by the

---

12. Mitchell, "Trinity of Themes," 74.
13. Tertullian, "Resurrection of the Flesh," 551.

CHAPTER 3: SETTING THE SPACE FOR EASTER CONVERSATION

Spirit; the flesh feeds on the body and blood of Christ, that the soul likewise may fatten on its God. [14]

Baptism welcomes us back onto the path of being more fully human in a manner exemplified in Jesus as he lived our humanity before us. That welcome begins with the church's ministry of baptismal preparation, making it clear that the grace of baptism does nothing to minimize our humanity, much less escape from it. Rather, baptism engages our bodily existence with a richness and intensity only made possible by the grace of God. For grace makes possible the reconciling of spirit and flesh, soul and body, as the non-negotiable criteria for a fully human life as God created it.

Several years ago, the congregation I serve was actively engaged with questions about our bodily participation in sacramental worship. To facilitate our conversation, I wrote this reflection:

> It is not the soul alone that makes us human;
>   without the body we are a mere wisp, if that.
> Care for human beings begins in the liturgy
>   where we are embraced, washed, fed,
>   and brought to our feet (as well as our knees)
>   in awe and wonder
>   before a God who loves us always
>   and before we ever were.
> Such care as we are learning is a way of life
>   we consent to live by a choice
>   that is as much the result of Love's divine wooing
>   as it is our continuing surrender to such love.
>
> This "way" is a peculiar form of "embodied" knowledge
>   that enters muscle and ligament, skin and bone
>   before we ever conceptualize faith as "thought."
> Our common error is to locate faith's center of gravity
>   in the mind when, in fact,
>   faith is the relentless "doing" in the body over time
>   that which we have seen and heard in Jesus.

---

14. Ibid.

Though audacious, it is true nevertheless:
>   human beings can only reach full humanity
>   when we strive to reflect God's image in us—
>   which is a struggle not to be taken lightly,
>   since we live in a world
>   where value must continually be earned.
> In an achievement-oriented world,
>   even people are reduced to "commodities"—
>   having a worth that is gained or lost
>   according to one's "usefulness."
>
> Therefore, it is not possible to have such faith as imagined here—
>   a surrender in obedience to extravagant "love"—
>   that is not also active in cultural resistance.
> And—there can be no resistance without critical reflection
>   which identifies corrosive patterns
>   that weaken, disfigure, and distort such "love."
> To receive and share this "love"—
>   without regard for what it earns or produces
>   or yields for our benefit—
>   is what salvation entails.
>
> Salvation does not remove us from this world,
>   but plunges us more deeply into it
>   as we are converted to a God-given "humanness"
>   to be lived out daily.
> This "humanness" is nothing less than the same
>   as was made visible and offered us as gift
>   by the Triune God who took flesh in Jesus Christ.
> This is the "gift" for which the saints give praise, the angels sing,
>   and the whole creation resounds in "Amen."[15]

What the church does in baptism has to do with bodies. The body of believers called the church gathers with candidates around water, who, through water and the Spirit, are joined to Jesus Christ, whose own body was crucified yet raised from the grave. And now, by divine mystery, this body is given us as food, that we might be

---

15. A slightly different version was published as Batchelder, "Sacramental Liturgy."

more and more fully the body of Christ in the world. The circularity in this last statement cannot be helped. Faith's mystery is a labyrinth of its own that leads us ever more deeply into the life of the triune God. And we are pilgrims in it.

6. Cherish Symbols and Ritual

Symbols and ritual are necessary to usher us into the mystery of God. For God appeared to Moses in a burning bush, not as a theological treatise. When we baptize, we encounter the mystery and marvel of God with us, who, having become *as us* in our humanness, redeems us in our totality through Christ's living, dying, and rising. Such an encounter requires that we handle the fundamental materials of creation itself: water, oil, soil, grain, fruit, and fire. We participate in ordinary actions of a domestic nature: washing, caressing, touching, blessing, embracing. Accompanied by the holy words of God's promise, God gives of God's own life in baptism, a new birth into a living hope. On their own, our holy words would break under the magnitude of this weighty meaning. For this reason symbol and ritual are indispensable to the sacraments.

Preparation for baptism involves an encounter with this meaning. Therefore, it constitutes a beginning exploration of the symbols and rituals that enact baptism. For if they are an integral part of the grammar of baptismal meaning, they can hardly be left out of the process of preparation. Aidan Kavanagh has written that "baptized life is an ensemble life. To live it is to live deep in symbol, deep in meaning, deep in ritual."[16] It makes perfect sense, therefore, for this preparation process to invite parents and leaders to gather with a bowl of water present. It makes sense that this water is engaged in a way that coheres with what is done in baptism—the signing of the cross, for example. And, it makes sense that a lit candle, centrally placed, marks the space and time of this meeting. Through these symbols connections are made between God's grace, the lives of the gathered lives, and the beloved earth given us as our home.

---

16. Kavanagh, *Elements of Rite*, 86.

PART 1: SHAPING A NEW VISION

One of the marks of a sacramental community is its skill and wisdom with handling symbols. We cannot live without them, but not because we assign them magical properties. Quite the contrary, we grasp the connection between our God-blessed earth and our own earthiness as those formed by God from the earth's dust. What brings this world into a new and radical arrangement is that this God took into God's own self this same dust through the incarnation of Jesus. By this act, our relationship with the world's materiality is forever transformed. The incarnation, together with all God's creative acts, renders this world holy. By this same divine initiative, our own lives as spirited bodies (or embodied spirits) are validated and affirmed in all our earth-ness. As with creation itself, so our life with God begins in water. It makes perfect sense. Twentieth-century English poet Philip Larkin reflects upon this mystery in his poem "Water."

> If I were called in
> To construct a religion
> I should make use of water.
>
> Going to church
> Would entail a fording
> To dry, different clothes;
>
> My litany would employ
> Images of sousing,
> A furious devout drench,
>
> And I should raise in the east
> A glass of water
> Where any-angled light
> Would congregate endlessly.[17]

---

17. Larkin, "Water".

7. Pay Attention; Discern Readiness

In Reformed theology there is no such thing as an "emergency" baptism. The anxiety that drives the human impulse to get a child baptized before it is too late (whatever "late" might mean) is rooted in a medieval narrowing of baptismal meaning to the removal of sin and the rescue of the endangered infant. This has left a long history of distorted theology that has strayed far from the graciousness of God and human response. As churches live out the renewal of baptism, they discover how much more deeply they can engage themselves in discerning readiness. Thus, the timing of baptism ought to be thoughtfully considered alongside the preparedness of those who are making promises to God in the presence of the faith community. Readiness concerns not only baptismal candidates and their sponsors, but also the baptizing community as a whole. The church itself is changed each time it gathers at the font to welcome another in Christ. As Mark Searle says, "It takes only one person to be baptized and all relationships are (in principle) altered."[18]

The Gospel of Jesus Christ sacramentally enacted in baptism is distorted when faith becomes all about the individual, when the church presents vows to those who have not been helped to live them, and when the church is not called to the costly giving of itself to seekers hungry for the Christ in the sacraments. The result is baptism's loss of meaning for us all and the loss of Gospel clarity in the world.

Rather than living within the abundant, untamed, and fecund waters of grace, we suffer spiritual drought. In addressing the matter of readiness, the Presbyterian "Directory for Worship" speaks of baptism "without undue haste, but without undue delay."[19] It is wise to ask what this looks like in the church's ministry. How does a church discern whether it has or has not been too hasty in its baptismal practice? Under what circumstances might a church discern delaying baptism so as to better attend to matters of formation and preparation? There is no single answer to such questions.

---

18. Quoted in Duggan, *Conversion and the Catechumenate*, 81.
19. PC(USA), *Book of Order*, W-2.3012a.

This is not a matter to be regulated. These questions make clear that this is a contextual matter and can be answered only with discernment rather than policy. What we seek to discern is readiness. Readiness is not a matter of possessing right answers to catechism questions. Readiness is a state of being before God, into which the church helps us grow. Readiness is nurtured in the company of others, attended to, and treated with patience and understanding. This explains why the process proposed in this book happens over time, without pressure, with lavish graciousness.

It all makes perfect sense when we envision faith as an organic, living reality rather than a set of beliefs. Many parents will have fresh memories of their nine-month pilgrimage to parenthood making ready themselves and their home for the new life of a child. Except in the most unusual circumstances, birth is not rushed. Birth comes in its own time when readiness is fulfilled and such time as this is quite different from the time of most convenience. In truth, pregnancy itself has nothing to do with convenience. Pregnancy involves sacrifice, imposition, disruption, and the near total reconfiguration of life. This is no less true with adoption. Both adoption and pregnancy embark parents on a journey for which the ending can only be glimpsed. Convenience can be an enemy to the spiritual readiness necessary for baptism whenever convenience imposes itself on the process. Celebrating baptism on the basis of family convenience can undercut the meaning of baptism, which is about a reality different from and much larger than an individual human family. Concerns for what is convenient can prove an interference when the timing of baptismal celebration is pulled towards family member schedules without regard for the church's festival days. This is because the meaning of baptism is enhanced and intensified when the celebration of baptism is timed with great baptismal feasts of the church. We might call this sacramental convergence. Such meaning comes together on the great baptismal festivals of the liturgical year: Easter, Pentecost, All Saints' Day, and Baptism of the Lord. It is wise, therefore, for churches to make broadly known the significance of these festivals

CHAPTER 3: SETTING THE SPACE FOR EASTER CONVERSATION

and to invite parents and families to reshape expectations around such high moments in the faith community's life.

By relaxing such external pressures as concern for personal convenience creates, participants are able to more freely give themselves to a process that seeks to cultivate the life of Christ in them. This deepening life of Christ in us is what leaders seek to recognize through prayer and discernment. The rush to baptism overlooks the important truth that preparation for baptism is part of baptism itself. Baptismal preparation and the act of baptism both share commonly in the grace of God that calls us, claims us, and conforms us to Christ. For this reason it is more helpful to speak in terms of Christian initiation, with the water bath of baptism being only one part. Indeed, can it not be said that gestation in the womb has an essential relationship with the day of birth? One is not possible without the other. So also, the time of preparation leading to the font is as much a part of baptism as the water washing itself. We do a great disservice to parents when the church deprives them of anything less than the best formational preparation possible. Sometimes this will mean that baptism will be celebrated at a time later than first expected.

What is possible without any delay is a ritual that many churches are choosing to practice. It is a newly recovered rite called "Thanksgiving for the Gift of Child."[20] Such a rite may be celebrated soon after a child's birth, providing parents with the opportunity, in the presence of the faith community, to express gratitude to God for their child and ask for God's blessing. Such a rite as this complements baptism, but does not replace it. Indeed, as part of what the church offers to parents in its preparation process, this rite can serve as a first step in an intentional process of baptismal preparation even as it provides a ritual possibility for a more immediate public response.

---

20. For examples of such a rite, see Archbishop's Council, *Common Worship*; Episcopal Church, *Book of Occasional Services, 2003*; Church of Scotland, *Welcome to a Child*, 1–23.

8. Involve Others; Enlist and Nurture Sponsors

It is the church that baptizes even when church polity designates that only persons ordained to particular service are authorized to preside at the sacrament. The liturgy itself bears witness to this truth. Through baptism, the church adds to its corporate body, which is Christ's own. With each baptism, the church is newly reborn. The church is enriched by the vitality that the newly baptized and their families bring to share in the church's life and ministry. Since there is one baptism and one alone, what is being said is no less true for the baptism of infants than adults. Yet, the deeper truth is that each baptism draws the whole of the baptizing body into the Spirit-filled process of ongoing conversion to Christ. Conversion is always communal, never individual, since each Christian remains forever a part of the larger whole. For this reason, the preparation process includes sponsors for the families bringing children to baptism.

Reformed theology has properly recovered the role of the whole church in baptism. This is clearly reflected in the promises made by the congregation at the time of baptism. In practice, however, the church's role as sponsor has been vague and ill-defined. Often the role of sponsors has been limited to standing alongside parents at the font. If this is all sponsorship entails, then it has become ritually cosmetic, a symbol of a relational ministry that does not exist. The process set forth here calls for the participation of committed and nurturing sponsors, carefully chosen, and called by God to this ministry. As this process takes form gradually in churches that commit to it, patience will be needed in the care and attention given to developing the ministry of sponsors.

Sponsors are not godparents. They are chosen by the church, not the parents. While some consideration ought to be given to relational complementarity, it is not wise to choose sponsors from the child's own immediate family. Since sponsorship is iconic of the new reality of relatedness into which we are born through baptism, the choice of a sponsor might well establish a relationship in the church on a new spiritual plane. What is most important is the willingness of sponsors to join parents as seekers with them. Sponsors are not chosen because they have the answers to theological questions. They are chosen because they possess gifts and character that cohere with the nature of this preparation ministry, namely hospitality, patience, understanding, and Christlike sympathy. Sponsors look out for parents and child, welcoming them each Lord's Day, making contact during the week when they are missed. Sponsors mediate the love and concern of the church in helping parents, as is often the case, establish a more regular participation in the worship and ministry of the church. Sponsors give themselves to parents in ways that are unmistakably genuine, never intrusive or manipulative. They share from their own faith experience and so become sources of reassurance to parents who easily feel overwhelmed and stressed by their new responsibilities. Through their companionship, offered according to the need of each parent, sponsors live out the answer of what it means to be church together. Such a ministry of making Christ visible as church presumes that even the most gifted of sponsors will benefit from training and orientation.

For too long, and with unfortunate consequences, churches have assumed that people are perfectly capable of filling the roles they are given with minimal explanation provided. We demean the ministries to which persons are called when we assume people can simply step in and serve without training. More than this, we deprive those we ask to serve of blessing. For each ministry in the church is practiced from a larger vision of God's dealings with us and our call in the world. When we take care to prepare people for the ministry of sponsorship, we invite them to see with new eyes their place in God's work and their new role with the baptismal candidate and family. Since sponsors are critical to the preparation process, they are an important focus of the church's attention.

9. Make Connections; Bring It Home

At one time, parents were led to think that their principle duty in "rearing children in the faith" was to bring them to Sunday school where they would receive a religious education. Though there was once a time when families in the Reformed faith practiced a disciplined faith in the home, today there is generally an absence of any communal expression of the faith in the family's home life. The church is responsible to lead in helping families recover the home as domestic church and empower parents as priests in their own homes. Surely one dimension of living out baptismal promises is the recovery of such a domestic liturgical life.

In the fall of 1992, more than five hundred leaders in the Presbyterian Church (USA) met in Chicago for a convocation titled "Discerning the Spirit, Envisioning Our Future." The design of this event called for participants to group themselves around those concerns for which each one felt a degree of passion. Over two hundred groups were formed, all representative of the concerns present in the denomination. The discussions of one such group, "Christian Nurture and Identity Formation," centered around the need to "nurture individuals so they affirm and claim their identity as members of God's covenant community." In considering the role of Sunday worship, along with the church's educational ministries, this group voiced concern for the family. It expressed:

> We have abandoned family as the locus of responsibility for Christian nurture. . . . How can we encourage faith formation in the context of the changing family? We need to provide resources that encourage families to worship/pray/celebrate through the week, and give them a starting point for doing so.[21]

Though new materials have been published to help parents nurture faith in the home, what remains largely undeveloped are resources that help build a liturgical home life *connected with* what takes place in the Sunday assembly. It is essential to bridge the worlds of home and church, and this is facilitated through the shared use of words, symbols, and rituals that help families live out a grateful awareness and call of the same baptismal identity that marks them when they gather on the Lord's Day.

---

21. PC(USA), General Assembly Council, *Discerning the Spirit*, 128.

CHAPTER 3: SETTING THE SPACE FOR EASTER CONVERSATION

This process seeks to equip parents in their roles as ritual-makers and as mystagogues. The process aims to establish in the home a pattern of festive worship that echoes the life of the assembly itself. The emphasis here is on the word "festive." Ritual festivity is intrinsic to all worship, without which ritual, song, silence, and symbol function only as printed texts that, according to Michael Warren, are not capable *by themselves* of giving an account of the new life given us in Jesus Christ.[22] In the absence of genuine festivity, our children will experience their parents' efforts to communicate the faith as a kind of indoctrination that takes the living faith out of its natural celebratory habitat. All faith born from the font is eucharistic; it is a grateful and heartfelt thanksgiving for overflowing grace unearned and undeserved. When festivity as joyful enactment is absent in church and home, what often emerges out of efforts to communicate the faith is compulsion. Many have painful childhood memories from well-meaning parents who force-fed their children a faith that was joyless, obligatory, and cast from a system of reward and punishment. Understandably, younger parents have reacted against such personal experience, wanting their own children to be free of such "baggage." Rather than offering nothing, the process outlined in this book intends to kindle a new vision, ignite a spark, generate life-giving expectations, and teach skills that will help parents become the architects of a festive liturgical life in the home.

The places to begin are at mealtime and bedtime. From the moment a newborn is taken into the home environment, he or she becomes alert and aware of its images, movements, smells, and sounds. The growing child learns much about his or her new family at mealtime and bedtime, at the family table and in the bedroom. These are conducive to ritual and natural places of beginning. Drawing upon the church's own communal liturgies of daily prayer and service for the Lord's Day, parents are able to root their family communal life in acts of praise, thanksgiving, and prayer. There is no need to "teach" in the formal sense of that word. Simply living this ritual out in the presence of young eyes and ears, with

---

22. Warren, *Faith, Culture, and the Worshiping Community*, 50–51.

an ink blotter mind that takes everything in, will shape a child's imagination. We should remember that participation precedes comprehension. Dorothy Coddington wisely advises, "I prefer to cut children's spiritual garments a little large, in order for them to grow up into, as they will in time. And who knows what vivid image or hint of the beauty of God may remain in their mind or memory?"[23] Coddington's wisdom counsels parents against a compulsiveness that children must achieve a particular stage of development before they are introduced to liturgical experiences. Consider how we introduce our children to books. Regularly, parents and grandparents read words that lie beyond a child's understanding in the moment. We trust that the repetition of word sounds over many hearings, together with colorful images, will slowly build a meaningful relationship between a child and the words. Additionally, this understanding is attended with emotion since the words and pictures arise from a relationship of unquestioned trust, love, and kindness. In the same way, ritual worship in the home can form meaningful faith in families.

10. Shape the Sunday Liturgy to Welcome All the Baptized

What has been said of liturgy in the home is no less true for the Sunday assembly. The service for the Lord's Day also ought to take the mode of festivity. Festivity is often mistaken as the confection of good feeling. Nothing could be further from the truth. Liturgical festivity is the form worship takes when prayer and praise makes extravagant and reverent use of ritual and employs powerful symbols that drip with meaning. Liturgical festivity engages all the body's senses, inviting movement and gesture, treasuring periods of intentional silence, and welcoming all present to participate as fully as possible. Anything less threatens to disconnect what children experience at home, especially if Sunday

---

23. Baker, Kaehler, and Mazar, eds., *Lent Sourcebook*, 12.

CHAPTER 3: SETTING THE SPACE FOR EASTER CONVERSATION

worship tends toward the more cerebral, cognitive, intellectual, passive, and verbal.

Robert Hovda writes:

> Good liturgical celebration, like a parable, takes us by the hair of our heads, lifts us momentarily out of the cesspool of injustice we call home, puts us in the promised and challenging reign of God, where we are treated like we have never been treated before anywhere else where we are bowed to and sprinkled and censed and kissed and touched and where we share equally among all a holy food and drink.[24]

The process proposed here is shaped to prepare parents and child for full initiation into Christ and his body, the church. This means not only the water bath in the triune name of God; it includes the laying on of hands and anointing with oil accompanied by the words of "sealing." Presenting a lighted candle to the newly illumined makes clearer the sacramental meaning of baptism. And it leads to the Lord's Table for the child's first Eucharist in the assembly, where she or he has become sister or brother in Christ. For life begun in the font is nurtured at the Table where the same Christ feeds us with himself.

The communing of newly baptized infants and children will challenge long-held and misguided attitudes among the Reformed. As with many theological biases, to fence off the Table until children are capable of understanding sacramental meaning is to privilege a cognitive understanding of Holy Communion and contribute to a false notion of faith as information. What is neglected is the affective hemisphere of the human brain. Who of us ever "understands" God's gracious encounters in the sacraments? The sacraments are not meant to be explained, but rather experienced. Mystery is encountered, not explicated. Even Calvin confessed as much when he wrote, "I will not be ashamed to confess that it is too high a mystery either for my mind to comprehend or my words to express; and to speak more plainly I rather feel than

---

24. Hovda, *Amen Corner*, 220.

understand it."²⁵ Thus, we grow into richer and fuller experience of sacramental meaning as we participate within the community of faith, rather than look on from the outside or suffer excommunication by being dismissed to an alternative age-specific program. Congregations that practice a generous welcome to children that includes the Lord's Supper testify to a deepening sense of belonging, wonder, and joyful delight in their full, conscious, and active participation.

11. Reimagine All Christian Education as "Formation for Baptismal Living"

In 1965, a Presbyterian scholar named C. Ellis Nelson delivered a series of lectures at Union Theological Seminary in Richmond, Virginia, calling the church to new challenges emerging in a changing world. His words would later be published in a book that explored important questions about the nature of faith—what it is and how it grows. He titled the book *Where Faith Begins*. Nelson's very first words in the Preface were these:

> Christians tend to think of the communication of religion in terms of the doctrines that should be explained. . . . This [book's] main contention is that religion at its deepest levels is located within a person's sentiments and is the result of the way he [sic] was socialized by the adults who cared for him as a child. The vital question we need to answer is "How does a person develop trust in the God revealed to us in the Bible—particularly in Jesus Christ—and what does that faith mean in his life?"²⁶

Nelson's question lies at the heart of baptismal faith. In baptism we ask, "Will you be Christ's faithful disciple, obeying his Word and showing his love, to your life's end?" The church is responsible to help people not only understand, but *live* what this means. The church is called to *show* people this meaning by demonstrating in

---

25. Calvin, *Institutes of Christian Religion*, 4.17.32.
26. Nelson, *Where Faith Begins*, 9.

CHAPTER 3: SETTING THE SPACE FOR EASTER CONVERSATION

its common life what such discipleship looks like. What we hear in Nelson's opening paragraph is a shift in perspective to a more thorough, comprehensive, and holistic vision of passing on the faith to others.

It is much more common now in Christian circles to hear a vocabulary shift in the way churches speak of their ministry. This new language can be accounted for by paying attention to the new perspective evidenced in Nelson's lecture forty-five years ago. Faith is less "taught" (as we think of the conventional teaching we received in public school education) and is more "formed" in us through experience and learned practices that mark the way Christians live in the world. The language of "faith formation" is more helpful to churches of the new millennium because it evokes a deeper and more expansive vision of how we nurture a growing faith in all ages. While this does not diminish the need to "educate" people in Bible knowledge, creedal statements, and church history, it does signal a deeper and more urgent concern to equip people with the life skills that will help them live faithfully as disciples. Knowledge alone conveys the misguided idea that faith consists in knowing the right answers. Nelson writes that "faith is an experience that can be thought about but *cannot be produced* by thinking. It is like hope and love in that it comes into our being through our associations and is strengthened through experience in our daily living."[27] Since ideas are born from language, a change in how we speak is necessary for grasping a new vision of ministry. Nelson had the prophetic insight to see that the changing cultural environment requires that the church adapt its educational ministry to new challenges.

Since Vatican II, much attention has been given the ancient catechumenate. Many churches are now adapting this ancient model in ways similar to the Rite of Christian Initiation of Adults (RCIA). This has fostered much scholarly ecumenical work researching and probing the theology and practice of the catechumenate. In his study of conversion in the early church, Alan Kreider identified three distinct but related aspects: belief, belonging, and

---

27. Ibid.,104. Italics added.

behaving.[28] The relationship between them becomes constitutive of what it means to have faith. Prior to the Christianization of the Roman Empire under Emperor Constantine, becoming a Christian first meant a relationship of belonging, from which new behaviors developed, with an attending embrace of the theological tenets of the church. This order changed under Constantine. Primacy was given to the church's beliefs. In this context, arguments over orthodoxy dominated a long historical period where faith became understood as the heartfelt assent to the official teaching of the church. Living, as we do, in a time of Christianity's decline and its displacement from its prior role of privilege in American culture, faith is re-emerging according to a pattern of belonging, behaving, then believing. More recently, Diana Butler Bass has written about the shift among people from "what" questions to "how" and "why" questions. This development signals a shift from an institutional understanding of faith to one that is fundamentally experiential. In her book *Christianity After Religion*, Bass joins a growing chorus of voices calling for the cultivation of intentional spiritual practices that deepen trust, foster discipleship, and draw out the deep meaning of who we are gifted and called to be in baptism.[29] This book coheres with that vision.

12. Live the Journey: Practice Baptismal Renewal and All Its Implications for the Church

What is being proposed invites readers to an alternative way of being church. Consider what difference a generous hospitality, enlivened imagination, and love for questions might mean in the practice of ministry. What might it mean for churches to embrace symbol and ritual, discern readiness, nurture sponsors, and connect the home to the Sunday liturgy? Doing so will open the church to new insights and possibilities for transformation in everything else the church is and does. To practice this ministry as

---

28. Kreider, *Change of Conversion*, xv.
29. See Bass, *Christianity After Religion*.

CHAPTER 3: SETTING THE SPACE FOR EASTER CONVERSATION

something separate or compartmentalized risks creating a spiritually elite that can be alienating. It is important to find ways for the blessing and vitality of this ministry to be shared in other ministries of the church. For this process can be the beginning of a new ecclesiology, centered in the sacraments, leading churches to an entirely different orientation from the ways ministry has functioned within the living memory of its members. This is why we may speak of this baptismal preparation process as a mustard-seed ministry; it begins small and grows, reorienting congregations around bath, pulpit, and table. No leader can know ahead of time what questions, challenges, and epiphanies will arise as a church begins this ministry. What can be assured is that people will find faith renewed, enlarged, and stirred in exciting ways as they are drawn nearer to the mystery of baptismal identity. This ministry is the beginning of a new journey for each church that undertakes it.

Summary

Taken together, these twelve "matters of primary concern" constitute a way of being church that does not require a new inventiveness but instead involves recovering a forgotten way of being church.

In a letter written at the time of the Second Vatican Council, liturgical theologian Romano Guardini reflected that it is not enough simply for the church to have new rites and improved rituals. The church must "re-learn a forgotten way of doing things and recapture lost attitudes."[30] This is true for all churches. We need to recover skills, rekindle senses, and rediscover, as essential, ways of apprehending the mystery of God that have suffered serious atrophy. The way we come to baptismal water, the response we make to nurture the hungry of heart, and the manner in which we live our lives from this water require that we relearn a forgotten way of being church. The proposal set forth in this book belongs to such recovery.

30. "Images in Worship," in Searle, *Visions*, 28.

PART 1: SHAPING A NEW VISION

Children's author Douglas Wood has written a story, *Old Turtle and the Broken Truth*, which I regard as a parable of the ministry presented in these pages. Long ago, in a time beyond reckoning, "in a land where every stone was a teacher and every breeze a language, where every lake was a mirror and every tree a ladder to the stars," there fell a truth "but as it fell it broke." The earth's creatures were drawn with curious fascination. Then, a bearer of the divine image—a human being—found the truth and read the writing. It said, "You are loved." The truth filled the human community with joy. Over time, "it became their most important possession." But, eventually, there came a day when the people "did not listen or hear the breezes and stones but heard only their truth. And they called it *the* truth." Feeling themselves good and proud and strong, they began to fear those who did not share their truth. Battles were fought and won over this truth and all creation suffered until the day came when a little girl, having had enough of the suffering, decided to visit Old Turtle to see what could be done. She journeyed far and long. She crossed the "Mountains of Imagining" and the "River of Wondering Why" and journeyed through the "Forest of Finding Out." When she grew tired her animal companions would carry her on their backs. When finally she met Old Turtle she poured out her heart over the suffering of the earth and its distressing conflict caused by the truth. This is what Old Turtle said: "It is because the broken truth is so close to a great, whole truth that it has such beauty and that the people love it so. It is the lost portion of that broken truth that the people need if the world is to be made whole again."

What follows in Part 2 is an aid to help churches navigate the "Mountains of Imagining," the "River of Wondering Why," and the "Forest of Finding Out."

Part 2:
Learning a New Practice

Introduction

THERE IS AN UNAVOIDABLE, but necessary, risk in setting forth, as I am doing, a specific model for prebaptismal preparation. The risk lies in the fact that we have been schooled in a curriculum-dependent educational system that is heavily dependent on educational materials. The danger lies in an overconfidence that fruitful understanding is achieved in relation to the quality of such resources. It is true that our choices of learning aids make a significant difference. Yet, such learning tools are only beneficial when placed in the hands of those who know that teaching is more a relational giving and receiving than a transmission of content. Thus, resources (such as are suggested here) are valuable only insofar as we learn to use them while also cultivating our instincts for wonder and awe, silence and space, mystery and grace. The church's ministry of catechesis, described in this book as *faith formation*, is best envisioned as the skillful work of a craftsperson. This section offers readers the experience of learning this craft by the doing of it. For this purpose, resources are offered that provide a pattern and path along with instruction for how to do the craft of baptismal preparation.

These resources have been developed over several decades of use. Over that time, I have experienced a broadening and deepening of insight and understanding in response to what participants have shared with me. As a result, the resources, as well as the pedagogy undergirding them, have evolved. Yet, however helpful these resources have been, it is the refinement of skills

PART 2: A MODEL OF SACRAMENTAL PREPARATION

essential to cultivating conversation that lies at the heart of this preparation process.

Practitioners eager to experiment with this preparation process are encouraged to trust themselves with the guidance offered here and to discover, from inside the experience, the newness awaiting them. It may be helpful for readers to think in terms of "inhabiting" the process. This involves a commitment to live out the pattern of the various sessions and their conversation pieces and taking time to reflect on the experience afterward. Such inhabiting asks that we make ourselves vulnerable to each session experience as it unfolds. As we do, we will taste and see the goodness of God in a meeting with others that bears resemblance to "Easter conversations" described in Part 1.

Now that I have made a case for trusting the guidance offered with each session, I want to stress the importance of remaining open to the gift of surprise, which can come in many disguises. In a culture that prizes preparation, management, and control, many of us prefer not being surprised. Yet, it is the nature of God to break into our tightly managed lives to bring from outside a newness that refreshes, challenges, confronts, and consoles. Surprise, by its nature, is experienced as unexpected. Since surprise belongs to the realm of the unforeseen, we do not plan surprise without the risk of it feeling contrived. As mentioned, surprises come in unforeseen ways including interruptions, distractions, objections, the release of emotion, and an off-topic comment that becomes a rabbit trail. The responsibility of leadership usually inclines us to resist surprise as an intrusion rather than to receive it as a potential moment of truthful disclosure. Since preparation for baptism is about becoming fully present to God's gracious gift in all our brokenness, moments of surprise can lead to profound transformation. Easter conversations are careful to not prematurely judge a session based on how we think it is supposed to go, lest surprises that might seem distracting be brushed over and missed as moments of pregnant possibility. Therefore, this process encourages an attitude of openness and alertness to surprises, which may take form in an off-the-wall comment or a question out of left field.

INTRODUCTION

Leaders should pay attention to a sudden change of someone's emotion, the evidence of tears or burst of laughter, moments of vulnerability, or declaration of disbelief. All such reactions and responses are possible, because this process is not about ideas of God, but the indwelling of God.

Leaders will always be challenged by surprises because we are presented with a choice. We can choose to enfold the surprise into the group experience and give it space, or we can plow ahead so as to stay on track. Wise are those who provide hospitality for surprise and its potential blessing. Wise are those who value as holy all that people share from their life experience, even when there seems no apparent connection to what the group has been talking about. If our orientation in Easter conversation is truly open to the untimed and unexpected, we will be of a better mind to consider how the mystery of God may be at work in our midst.

I have mentioned the importance of taking time to reflect on the shared experience after each session even making personal notes for later reference. This kind of reflection helps to surface and preserve insights that we cannot easily recognize in the midst of the ongoing experience.

Moreover, leaders will find the value of this reflection deepened if we do this with others, perhaps sponsors, assisting in the process. Reflecting with others helps us come to depths of insight and levels of clarity that we could not reach alone. The practice of such reflection is central to learning the artistry of Easter conversation.

Intentionality is important with everything related to this baptismal preparation process. Intentionality might be defined as forethought with what will be done, why it will be done, how it will be done, and how the "what, why, and how" are congruent with fundamental faith convictions. When we act from intention, we reduce the distance between our feelings, motives, and understandings so that our actions reveal a certain integrity. Leading from intention helps leaders to be more fully present for others and less preoccupied (and, therefore, distracted) with themselves.

PART 2: A MODEL OF SACRAMENTAL PREPARATION

To enhance such intention, leaders will find it helpful to take time prior to each session for the following:

1. Spend enough time with the design and flow of each session to grasp the whole in relation to its parts. Each individual session, as with the whole process itself, is part of a movement in faith that can be considered a kind of pilgrimage. With each gathering, participants journey into the mystery of God's gracious dealings with humanity, a journey where leaders serve as guides. In preparation, leaders are wise to ask: in what direction is this process leading?

2. Take care to prepare the physical space where the session will take place. Even spaces initially judged to be mediocre can be improved in ways that can enhance the group experience. Perhaps there are sponsors who might be willing to come early and give assistance. As tables and chairs are rearranged and objects are set in place, take the opportunity to discuss with sponsors the hopes for the coming session. Such conversation helps sponsors to see a relation between the room design and the formation intention of the sessions. Remember that preparing space should touch all matters of hospitality as noted in Part 1: comfort of chairs, visual and/or audible distractions, room temperature, lighting, food, beverage, etc. It is wise to double-check on all that is needed so that no one needs to leave the session for something that was forgotten.

3. Place a substantial candle in the center of the group where it will be prominently seen by all. A white candle two and a half to three inches wide and of modest height would do well, and is inexpensive to purchase. Lighting the candle at each session is a kind of ritual invocation, and reinforces a sense that the place of gathering is holy ground. In addition, set out water in a glass bowl so that it is visible to all. The presence of water during the sessions enriches the conversations that will take place. After all, baptism is about God's gracious acting through material signs, water being indispensable to all life.

INTRODUCTION

As will be seen below, this process intends that water be used ritually within each preparation session.

4. Prepare copies in advance for participants' texts and resources suggested for each session. It may be helpful to give participants a folder or binder so that the pages are not misplaced and can be brought to subsequent sessions. The value of distributing resources is so that each participant can spend time later on his or her own reflection following the session. A binder will help participants preserve materials for continued use and reflection as part of each one's ongoing formation in faith.

5. Decide how and where to adapt a session according to particular group dynamics and need, for there are likely more suggestions offered in each session than time will allow. Be wisely selective and avoid the temptation of trying to do everything if it appears to be more than possible. Completing the material is not the point; it never is. These resources are suggestive, offering guidance, but they must be adapted locally as each situation warrants. Leaders are responsible to make judgements on what to bypass or save for later. It may be best that a particular session to be skipped altogether based on what is possible in a local congregation. As mentioned in Part 1, churches beginning to use this process may not be able to do all six sessions. Local leadership is best positioned to make such decisions. After all, no one knows a local ministry context better than resident leaders. Learn to do a little well before trying to undertake too much. There will be opportunities for more if people find their lives enriched with what has been offered them. Indeed, the process of living into our baptism remains unfinished throughout our lives and is only completed in death. This process is a way of opening up to a fullness of grace discovered in relationship with God, others, and the world. If it is not feasible to use all the sessions presented here during a particular period of preparation, leaders may consider using these resources

as part of their church's ministry with families and young children. In this regard, be creative and think out of the box, giving thanks for the spiritual hunger evident in those who respond. Those sessions not used with a first child might be incorporated into a second process when a family is gifted with its second or third child. Indeed, experience teaches that there is much to be gained by using these resources over again with families having more than one child. We do not remain the same. Time and experience change us. Parents returning for the baptism of a child born years later have new insight and readiness that will provide for meaningful conversation. I have heard parents comment on how valuable it was for them to go through the process again. One mother shared that it might be worth having another child just to experience the richness of this preparation process.

Session 1:
The Gift of a Child and the Journey of Faith

Opening Ritual

PLACE A CANDLE IN the center of the table with a small bowl of water. Welcome each person as he or she arrives. After all are gathered in a room suitably prepared, request that cell phones be put on vibrate or, better yet if all can agree, turned off. This way of beginning helps to keep at arms length the many things of life that want to command our attention. Such boundary setting has become more difficult with the omnipresence of digital devices. In committing to such a practice as part of baptismal preparation, we make possible a contemplative oasis for those present and teach a small discipline that can help guard family time in the home.

Now begin a minute of silence to allow all to center their minds and hearts with a sense of holy expectation for what will unfold. After a minute, someone previously designated lights the candle. The match striking the box may be the sound that breaks the silence; the flash of combustion and transfer of flame to wick captures the groups gaze, fusing the focus in a simple symbolic act. The deliberateness in the act of candlelighting need not be accompanied by speech. The action speaks for itself. Indeed, the silence that precedes adds intensity to the power of the symbols being used in the ritual act. This ritual gesture has ancient roots in the church's life of worship and prayer, as well as for families gathering at table for the evening meal in their homes. The candle, having been lit, is followed by words of greeting borrowed from the church's liturgy.

> The leader says: *The grace of our Lord Jesus Christ be with you all.*
>
> The people respond: ***And also with you.***

To hear the language of the liturgy in contexts other than Sunday worship will form an impression on those gathered. At the very least, it will suggest that the reality associated with these words is no less true in this unfolding moment than when so many more are assembled for worship. There is an important connection to be made, which can be named at some later session, that who we are in this small group gathering is no less than who we are when we gather with many others for Sunday worship. It is an identity of common belonging and calling. Since baptismal preparation is about a gifted identity, the use of language more commonly experienced in the weekly liturgy can stir participants to think at new depths in the faith. Furthermore, such words of greeting, used at the start of each session, model a pattern as appropriate for a family at home as when all are gathered at Sunday worship. This parallel between church and home is what undergirds the affirmation of the home as "domestic church."

Personal Faith in Relationship to the Birth of a Child

The theological affirmation on which Session 1 rests is that God is continually "up to something" in and with our lives. God's claim does not violate the freedom given to each of us, nevertheless, God gently and persistently courts our response to grace that is unearned, undeserved, and frequently unrecognized. Based on these convictions, Session 1 begins with these questions: "How did we get here—to this meeting—on this subject—baptism?" "Is my participation in this process only accountable to a decision I am making to have my child baptized, or is there something *more* going on?" "Might these meetings having to do with baptizing children

SESSION 1: THE GIFT OF A CHILD AND THE JOURNEY OF FAITH

also be a meeting between God and me, as a parent, and be an opportunity for me to make a fresh inquiry into what baptism—*my own baptism*—might mean in my life now?" These questions suggest there is much more going on than meets the eye. They invite each participant to receive these preparation sessions as a fresh opportunity to consider God in each one's personal life.

The offer must be invitational; there can be nothing manipulative or coercive in word or tone. No one should be made to feel that her or his current status with God is being judged. What good purpose would that serve? Consider the image Jesus gives of the younger son returning home in shame, expecting to be demoted in the family, yet being received with love and affirmation of belonging.

The birth of a child frequently brings back to church people who were once more active in the church's life but, for whatever reasons, have ceased to participate with regularity. They may have fallen out of practice with those activities that feed a personal faith. Or, it may be they were never formed in such disciplines as Scripture reading, personal prayer, and meditation. Many years may have come and gone since new parents were active at church. All of this is possible, since it is known that the birth of a child is often an experience that stirs a seemingly dormant faith among parents. Session 1 does not begin with a person's *past*. The past, whatever it might have been, may at some later time need to be explored, but this will reveal itself should it be necessary. Moreover, the most suitable place for a leader to visit with someone's past will be in private conversation within the protection of confidentiality. Session 1 begins with the *present* by affirming the compelling truth that we are always coming to God anew, bringing a past that has need of forgiveness, reconciliation, and redemption because God is continually at work to make us new creatures in Christ. The attention, therefore, is given to the present opportunity to which everyone has made time in their schedules to share in conversation occasioned by a desire for baptism. It is no less than a *kairos* moment where God is drawing us all into the breadth of God's purpose. That *this* meeting together around baptism has come to be is no small thing. It is evidence of a hunger for God. And wherever there is such hunger, God is near.

PART 2: A MODEL OF SACRAMENTAL PREPARATION

It is pastorally wise and theologically sound to regard each one's desire for a child's baptism as a stirring from God. That is the starting point. Even if it appears that someone is requesting baptism from pressure (perhaps coming from relatives), no one knows what measure of awakening and conversion might be experienced as the baptismal preparation unfolds. We should assume the Holy Spirit's presence as an active agent calling us all to deeper faith and commitment. Where the process leads from Session 1 will always remain to be seen, but as a place of beginning, it is pregnant with possibility. Therefore, Session 1, as an introduction to all other sessions, presents a way of having conversation about God and faith. For this purpose, it uses the image provided below.[1]

1. This image appears in the book *Encyclopedia of Serendipity* (p. 73), by Lyman Coleman, and is used here with the author's permission. In personal correspondence with me he wrote that the picture was given to him as a gift in 1968 by a priest at Xaverian High School in Brooklyn, New York.

SESSION 1: THE GIFT OF A CHILD AND THE JOURNEY OF FAITH

This drawing is an effective way for each participant to *read* her or his life spiritually. Engaging this picture helps each one come to a sense of personal recognition about one's own relationship with God as it is at the moment. Here are some possible words with which leaders might introduce this exercise:

> We are present together in response to your desire to seek baptism for your children. Your presence is a response to the impulse of faith occasioned by the birth of a child. The gift of a child can be thought of as an awakening on many levels.
>
> Parents, consider how alive you have become to life, the world, and each other since your child first came into this world. Consider how alert your senses have become—the smell of your child, the touch of his/her skin, the sound of his/her cooing and crying, your feelings when your eyes meet. With a child comes newness in abundance. Such awakening extends to our spiritual lives, nudging us to ask questions about our life with God, and how God is at work now giving us the gift of a child. As we think about preparing to take baptismal vows, it is helpful to ponder how we see ourselves in relation to God at this moment. Take a look at the picture provided here. Imagine this tree as the Christian faith. As you think about your life of faith, with which child do you most identify, and why?

After ninety or so seconds, leaders should invite participants to share as they choose, making sure they know they are also free to pass if they prefer. This sharing should not be hurried. As the first experience of group sharing, it lays the groundwork for all that is to come. Do not be surprised if someone identifies with more than one child from the picture. When appropriate, help participants see that there are no value judgments implied by the picture. There is no inherent hierarchy of spirituality or commitment. For example, higher up in the tree does not equate to greater achievement. Many different interpretations are possible depending on how a person reads her or his own experience into the sketch. This is the beauty of it. Thus, there are no right or wrong answers, only authentic responses to be made. Our hope is that participants will be free to see their lives before God as "works in process." This freedom includes recognizing that life with God is not about adherence to religious rules. Rather, life, begun in baptism, consists of our ongoing response to grace-filled moments of new possibility that enter our lives in all kinds of surprising ways.

After sharing around the question, "With which child do you most identify in terms of your relationship with God?" leaders might tweak the question just a bit to ask, "Where would you *like to be* in this picture? Would you choose a different child, and why?" Be sure to allow time for participants to reflect as it will help them dig deeply into their awareness of personal faith. By continuing to engage participants with picture and questions, leaders will find themselves facilitating a spiritual conversation of honest disclosure in a setting that is gracious, forgiving, and loving. How long has it been, we might wonder, since those participating have had such an experience? The power of questions rests in how they bring to consciousness the hidden longing for God within each of us.

Depending on time and comfort level, leaders may consider extending this engagement with the picture a little longer. Consider asking the following: "Imagine this tree as Christian *parenthood*, that is, the challenge of nurturing your child's faith. Where do you see yourself as a parent? With which child do you identify?" Once again, allow time to ponder. The purpose of inquiry is to help parents name their anxieties about *being* parents and taking spiritual responsibility for their children. Through such sharing, each parent will see that he or she is not alone with these feelings. Helping participants to name their emotions will cultivate their readiness for the sessions themselves, since the intent of the preparation process is to guide and form them to undertake this responsibility. What is offered below is one way to introduce this stage of reflection.

> What if I said that there are not two trees but one? What if I said that since the birth of your child the *tree of faith* and the *tree of parenthood* is one and the same tree. The

birth of a child comes as God's gift to us. With gift comes calling. God's call to you is to live out the faith with a new identity as a parent. That's what it means to say yes to the question asked at baptism: *Do you promise to live the Christian faith and teach that faith to your child?* In becoming a parent, you have entered a life different from before; you have been made new with the gift of your child. While marriage/partnership and parenthood do not comprise all of who you are, it is a significant part of your new *identity and life context* in which you now live the faith.

Why Water?

The second part of this session moves the group from a time of personal sharing into a reflection on the meaning of baptism. In times past, the church's instruction in the sacraments has centered itself in confessional and doctrinal statements, sometimes accompanied with Scripture. There is a useful place for this material, but not as a place to start. The sacraments make use of material signs, says John Calvin, because God condescends to human weakness.[2] That is, God chooses to communicate in those forms and ways that are readily accessible for our understanding and apprehension. It is far more helpful, therefore, to begin an exploration of baptism with water itself. This process begins with the question, "Why water?"

Taking into her or his hands the bowl of water already set out for all to see, the leader asks participants, "What are the most common ways you encounter water in your life?" This is a simple question asking people to name the many ways water is a part of our lives. Only a brief time is necessary for sharing, just enough to get the mental gears in motion. Next, distribute a handout prepared for this segment of the session. One can easily be made using text from this section of the session. Putting something into

---

2. See Calvin, "Short Treatise on the Supper," 58; Calvin, "Excerpt from 'Short Treatise on the Supper,'" 109.

PART 2: A MODEL OF SACRAMENTAL PREPARATION

participants' hands visually reinforces the spoken word and gives a way to extend personal reflection beyond the group session when participants are at home.

WHY WATER?

Christ's act in the church: Why does the church make new Christians with WATER?

In Marilynne Robinson's novel, Gilead, about a congregational minister's recollections to his young son, Reverend John Ames refers to a comment of Ludwig Feuerbach saying:

"Water is the purest, clearest of liquids, in virtue of this its natural character it is the image of the spotless nature of the Divine Spirit. In short, water has a significance in itself, as water; it is on account of its natural quality that it is consecrated and selected as the vehicle of the Holy Spirit. So far there lies at the foundation of Baptism a beautiful, profound natural significance."

Water is necessary to life.
Water is life-giving.
Water is death dealing.
Water cannot be tamed.
Water is thirst-quenching.
Water refreshes, cleanses, purifies, renews.

As a **natural element** so essential to all life, water - as a symbol - is capable of carrying the fullness of meaning associated with God's promise in baptism.

In baptism, there is
  death and resurrection
  washing of sin
  new birth
  incorporation into Christ

Thus, as the place of baptism, the font (from the Latin "spring") is
  a WOMB from which we are *reborn*
  a BATH where we are *washed and cleansed*
  a TOMB where we *die and are raised to new life*

Gilead.New York: Picador, 2004, 23, 24.
Image of Jesus' Baptism - David Bjorgen/Wikicommons/Public Domain

---

"*Why water? Christ's act in the church: Why does the church make new Christians with WATER?*" Begin this inquiry by reading the quotation below. It is taken from Marilynne Robinson's

SESSION 1: THE GIFT OF A CHILD AND THE JOURNEY OF FAITH

novel *Gilead*, about a congregational minister's recollections to his young son. In the book, Reverend John Ames refers to a comment of Ludwig Feuerbach:

> Water is the purest, clearest of liquids, in virtue of this its natural character it is the image of the spotless nature of the Divine Spirit. In short, water has a significance in itself, as water; it is on account of its natural quality that it is consecrated and selected as the vehicle of the Holy Spirit. So far there lies at the foundation of Baptism a beautiful, profound natural significance.[3]

As a natural substance so essential to all life, water as symbol, is capable of carrying the heavy weight of meaning associated with God's promise in baptism. Water is necessary to life.

It is life giving and death dealing. Water is thirst quenching, yet it cannot be tamed. Water refreshes, cleanses, purifies, and renews. More might be said, but these properties and powers of water help us answer the question, "Why water?" Everything we have named in relation to water is transposed to the meaning of baptism we encounter in Scripture, and in the sacramental tradition of the church. In baptism, there is death and resurrection, washing of sin, new birth, and incorporation into Christ's life and mission. For these reasons, the church holds in its memory a special language for the place of baptism. The container for baptismal water, the "font" (coming from the Latin *fons*, meaning "spring"), is spoken of as a *womb* from which we are reborn, a *bath* in which we are washed, and a *tomb* wherein we die and are raised to new life. This language helps us to see how the water of baptism is a symbol with many layers of meaning, no single meaning capturing the fullness of its mystery.

It is not necessary in this session to dive deeper into any of these images for baptism. It is enough for leaders simply to set them forth as affirmations without explanation. Rather, associating the meaning of baptism with the properties of water evokes relationships and experience that stir the imagination leaving participants

---

3. Robinson, *Gilead*, 23–24.

in a state of pondering. In later sessions, there will be time to delve more deeply as questions are asked and conversation leads.

Closing Ritual

It was stated earlier, in speaking about lighting a candle at the start of each session, that this preparation process was a coming together on holy ground. These sessions imagine more than a conversation *about* God and faith; they imagine the time as communion *with* God, present through the Holy Spirit, but also present in each participant. This conviction shapes the way each session concludes before all go their way. The parting ritual gestures these truths in a form that is both affirmation and blessing. Not only does this provide a kind of seal to the experience just shared, the ritual inscribes the truths shared on the bodies of all present. This is powerful; it is a God-moment bringing a shared awareness that the time together has been much more than expected, perhaps even hoped for.

The leader begins the ritual by taking the bowl of water and modeling the ritual action that will be replicated by each participant as the bowl is passed around the group. Turning to the person on the right, the leader makes the sign of the cross on forehead of that person and says, *"[First Name], remember your baptism and be thankful, you belong to God."* The one receiving the ritual signing then turns to his or her right and repeats the action so that it is carried around the entire circle. Think about it. In the time shared together, water was not only talked about in the conversation, it was present in a bowl throughout the session. This same water is now being put to holy use in an exchange of touching and being touched, with each person ministering and ministered to, in a grace-filled, gestured word of blessing. Each person will be drawn into another's gaze. Each will be vulnerable before another. Each will know the experience of giving and receiving. For many, it will be the first time to trace the sign of the cross, or have it traced on their bodies. There will be the sensation of being made wet, and it will linger for a time as the water slowly evaporates. Perhaps, even, a drop of water will find a path from forehead down

SESSION 1: THE GIFT OF A CHILD AND THE JOURNEY OF FAITH

the cheek—or it may be a tear. This ritual of closing has a power far beyond what we might imagine as it is written of here. Our bodies remember what ritual inscribes; ritual is "a way of thinking with the skin."[4] In my congregation, parents who participated in baptismal preparation continued this watery signing ritual with their children at home as a way of nightly blessing. These same children, now years older, regularly conclude their Sunday formation time with the same ritual blessing, remembering their baptism and being thankful.

So will be the way of closing with each preparation session, and in so doing leaders will cultivate a ritual competence in participants. By competence I mean familiarity and comfort, which translates into doing something ritually so that we feel at home saying words, doing gestures, and handling symbols that speak of who by faith we are. Leaders are wise, therefore, to encourage families to experiment at home lighting a candle at their own meal tables, and setting out a small bowl of water to be passed so each may trace a watery sign of the cross on the forehead. This is how we are formed from the inside out. "Teach your body and your body will teach your soul."[5] Over time, participants will be formed in a new way of living the faith that does not reside in the realm of beliefs and ideas about God. As a way of embodying the faith, it will help to make us whole.

After the water ritual is completed, the following prayer, or something similar, is prayed together (copies may be made for all):

> God of new beginnings,
>
> from a watery womb
>
> your Spirit birthed us to new life.
>
> Form us in the life of Christ, your Son,
>
> making us faithful as servants
>
> in all you call us;
>
> through Jesus Christ our Lord. **Amen.**

4. Mitchell, "Trinity of Themes," 73

5. This expression is a favorite of the Rev. Dr. Gláucia Vasconcelos Wilkey, friend, colleague, and liturgical theologian in the Presbyterian Church (USA).

Session 2: Prayer and Baptismal Life

Opening Ritual

Since each session begins by following the common pattern established in Session 1, it will be enough to recall here in outline form what was described earlier.

1. A candle is placed in center of table with a small bowl of water.
2. After all are gathered, a minute of silence is kept.
3. The candle is lit in silence by one of the participants.
4. The leader greets the group:

    The grace of our Lord Jesus Christ be with you all.

    The people respond: ***And also with you.***

Prayer as Our Native Tongue

Among the practices at the heart of baptismal life is prayer. Prayer is a practiced way of bringing as much of our lives as we can before as much of God as we know. What we bring to voice in prayer includes not only our personal lives, but the world at large, from which we can never be isolated. Prayer is one form through which

SESSION 2: PRAYER AND BAPTISMAL LIFE

"loving our neighbors as ourselves," including those oceans away, comes to expression.

While emotion informs and even infuses our praying, prayer is not dependent on feelings for its practice. This is because prayer is the heart's language, whether it takes form as praise, thanksgiving, confession, lament, petition, or intercession. All expressions of prayer are learned. Each of us is created with a yearning for God, and we learn to articulate that yearning by participating in a praying community. The ancient church regarded the liturgy as the "school of prayer" because the liturgy equipped Christians with the necessary vocabulary, syntax, structure, and grammar of which prayer is made. Every prayer offered by Christians, including those prayed in quiet solitude, are constitutive of the church's prayer, since every believer's prayer cannot be separate from the prayer of Christ's body of which each Christian is a member. Prayer, personal as well as communal, is a fundamental practice and expression of baptismal living. To be baptized is to be born into a life in communion with God; therefore, learning how to pray is critically important to growing up into our baptism.

Session 2 invites participants to reflect on these truths and to see the baptism of their child as an opportunity both to grow more fully as parents in the practice of prayer and to begin forming their newly baptized child in a life of prayer. These two intentions are implied by the vows parents undertake at baptism, and they are lived out in such a way that each is interwoven with the other.

Asked to pray, many adults must first swallow hard. It is commonly felt that praying out loud is what professionals do; most everyone else defers to the experts. One word describes what many feel at the thought of such a challenge: awkward. No one likes to feel awkward because it brings such intensity of self-consciousness that sweat glands activate and the pulse quickens. Those who might manage a prayer when asked to do so may find themself preoccupied with sounding appropriate to listeners and unable to focus on actually addressing God. This anxiety around praying is one manifestation of a process at work in North American Christianity over a very long time. There has been an increasing *interiorization* of spiritual experience so that faith is deemed as something felt and thought about, without necessarily coming to visible expression. At the same time, there is a growing cultural consensus that *sincerity* is the hallmark of authenticity. Furthermore, the supreme test of sincerity is originality, that is, it must come from the heart. In the case of prayer, many believe it must be offered from one's own words. Something borrowed and repeated is considered inferior because it does not meet the criteria of improvised speech. Together, these conspire against that natural predisposition children have for the role repetition plays in forming faith.

Forming the newly baptized in faith involves learning the language of the praying community into which one is incorporated through baptism. Session 2 invites participants to begin becoming fluent in the community's language of prayer, and it does this by suggesting that particular prayers be committed to memory through a regular practice of prayer in the home. The questions provided in this session help us to think about *how* we learn and the *value* of having prayer texts anchored in memory. What becomes clear is that set forms of prayer are a vital aid in learning how to pray, and the most accessible way to teach others to pray. The Easter conversation in this session sets forth the church's liturgy as the school of prayer.

Turning to the participants gathered in the room, the leader begins by asking, "What have you learned that you can recite from memory?" Common responses will include nursery rhymes, the Pledge of Allegiance, or a childhood song. The point of this question is to make participants aware that each has something she or he can recite without an aid. Next, the leaders asks, "From whom did you learn these words? What can you remember about first being taught these words?" These questions are more difficult and will take several minutes to think about. They ask the participants to access memories reaching back a long time, memories that may be inaccessible. The difficulty of remembering is the point of the question.

Many of us (perhaps most) are able to access a text of something planted in our memories, but from such an early age that we cannot retrieve a memory of having been taught it. Someone

SESSION 2: PRAYER AND BAPTISMAL LIFE

might answer, "I just know it! I think I must have learned it from my mother but I don't remember her teaching it to me." What such a response bears witness to is what it means to know something "by heart." While it is possible to learn something "by heart" at later ages by working to memorize a text, there is a special place for texts in our lives with which we have *no* memory of *not knowing*. Such knowing is beyond the reach of remembering when and how something was learned. This kind of knowing something holds a powerful place in our being because we can't remember a time in life when we did not know what we know.

Teaching children to pray through the regular practice of particular prayers is to place the language of baptismal faith in the deepest regions of a child's memory. This insight is what the questions in this session seek to make evident. The conversation made possible from these questions will reveal what a splendid opportunity parents have to teach the faith to their child from birth.

To advance the conversation, leaders may ask, "What language of faith—hymns, prayers, Bible verses—are you able to recite from memory? In what settings do you remember hearing these words?" Fewer of us will be able to recall texts of a religious nature so deeply embedded in our memory. Persons may recall a version of the Lord's Prayer or a verse from a hymn. Additional probing might ask, "From whom did you learn these words? On whose lips do you remember first hearing these words?" The use of questions, as here in this session, is to lead people to new understanding without dependence on "telling." Questions are most congenial to discovery. A truthful insight will be more powerfully experienced if it has "dawned" on someone, that is, come to light. Questions are far more effective than statements in helping people come to see what has hitherto been unknown to them.

The central conversation in Session 2 has to do with the relational transmission of faith. We learn faith as it is embodied by others for us. To bring this truth to light, leaders might ask, "When you pray, what words do you use? From whom or from where did you get these words? When you remember praying, what time of day or occasions come to mind?" All these questions raise awareness. Some will recall a prayer prayed at mealtime or bedtime. Others may have no such memory at all and may have a sense of deficit regarding their upbringing. Preparing for their child's baptism is an important time for parents because parents have an opportunity to shape a different home life for their child than what they experienced. With respect to faith practice in the home, many parents will be motivated by a desire to be more intentional about how they live their faith as a family. Such desire is what this preparation process seeks to instill. As participants realize the profound implications a child's baptism has for them, they will grow in eagerness for each successive session since the sessions are about equipping parents to fulfill the vows they make at baptism. The reason we teach children to pray from birth is because we have the unique opportunity to seed our children's hearts and minds with prayers that can serve them their whole lives. In order for us to give our children the wonderful gift of knowing prayer at the deepest level of memory, it will be necessary that we trust set forms of prayer that favor repetition and verse.

At this point in the conversation, it will be helpful for leaders to briefly share these insights from early childhood learning theory as it pertains to nurturing children in the faith:

1. What we learn at a *preliterate, precognitive* age is retained at the deepest level of the human person.

2. Only what is repeated can be so learned. *Repetition* is the vehicle through which the gift is given.

3. Rhyme and meter aid memory because of the musicality of the words and phrases.

4. Bedtimes and mealtimes are moments of high ritual intensity in which Christians have offered prayer. Such moments are ideally suited for family prayer.

5. When we add a symbol (e.g., a candle at mealtime and the sign of the cross at bedtime) we provide a richer texture to family worship by bringing speech, symbol, and gesture together.

The power of ritual lies in the way it marries doing with saying, action with words; this marriage forms the core of all worship, including worship in the home.

A Child's Capacity to Apprehend God and a Parent's Role as Fellow-learner

One of the presumptions underlying everything that has been suggested in this preparation process is that children are born with a capacity to apprehend God. Though the Gospel is not clear precisely why it is, children possess qualities that seem to atrophy in adulthood, leading Jesus to say that "whoever does not receive the kingdom of God as a little child will never enter it" (Luke 18:17 NRSV). Some have seen in children a capacity for the numinous. Constance Tarasar writes that the

> initial dependence and trust of the child is without constraints. The child has no fear that its needs will not be fulfilled; such a possibility has not yet been discerned. As the child's wants are supplied, a native trust develops that assures continual satisfaction whenever these needs arise. Is not this trust and dependence the kind of dependence and trust that Christ wants us to place in God?[1]

What this means is that in their child's baptism, parents are gifted to be co-disciples with their children, becoming fellow-learners of the faith with them. Rather than becoming intimidated by the challenge implicit in baptismal vows, parents who feel an acute sense of inadequacy should rejoice in the opportunity afforded them, through their children, of making a new start in the faith for themselves. Mark Searle believes that we do not so much promise to teach our children merely what we know as much as we promise to learn again anew the story with them. He writes, "It is chiefly by our living the Christian story, that our children will come to pick it up and to develop the skills necessary to be faithful to it."[2] This is a wonderful

---

1. Tarasar, "Taste and See," 46.
2. Searle, "Infant Baptism Reconsidered," 48–49.

way for leaders and participants to think about what baptism offers to a family; it is the opportunity for parents to enter the Christian story anew with their child, learning and living it together.

As parents attend to their family's faith, care should be taken to avoid overly simplistic, juvenile prayers. Prayers accessible to children should not be childish in language. There are no grade levels in the church's anthology of prayer. Since the prayers families first begin praying together at mealtimes and bedtimes are those that will rest most deeply in memory, choose wisely from the richness of the community's prayer life. As I first mentioned in the Introduction, Dorothy Coddington's wisdom bears repeating: "I prefer to cut children's spiritual garments a little large, for them to grow into, as they will in time. And who knows what vivid image or hint of the beauty of God may remain in their mind or memory?"[3] What this wisdom means is that we must not shortchange children but rather give them language they will grow into throughout their lives. There is great value in seeding their minds with words and phrases without expecting them to reach an immediate understanding. In time, children will grow up into the meaning of a prayer. Meanwhile, the prayer itself will be a life-long companion to the soul.

The quotes above from Mark Searle and Dorothy Coddington might be printed out for participants to take with them following the session for further reflection at a later time. There is much to think about and return to in both statements. Both Searle and Coddington address themselves to expectations. Both shape how parents might think about responding to their children's faith formation and learning to pray. It is not necessary for parents to have a certain command of spiritual knowledge before being competent to nurture their child's faith. As parents, we share our faith as we *live it out* with our children. We are learners together with children, coming to the faith anew and afresh as we learn with them.

---

3. Baker, Kaehler, and Mazar, *Lent Sourcebook*, 12.

Practice at Home

Since living out baptismal vows takes form in how families practice their faith in their homes, Session 2 encourages families to now begin the practice of mealtime and bedtime prayers as often as possible. Leaders can provide participants with the text from what follows. Invite parents to choose prayers from among the suggestions and pay attention to their own experience. Tell them there will be opportunity to share together at the next session.

Suggested Prayers for Mealtime

Lord Jesus be our holy guest,
our morning joy, our evening rest,
and with our daily bread impart,
your love and peace to every heart.[4]

Lord, you clothe the lilies,
you feed the birds of the sky,
you lead the lambs to pasture,
the deer to the waterside,
you multiplied loaves and fishes,
and changed the water to wine;
come to our table as giver
and as our guest to dine.[5]

God of holy table,
only you are able,
to give and bless
for you are host
and you are guest.

Flavor with love this meal,
fire our hearts with zeal,
your light to shine,
your peace to share,
as here with you we dine.[6]

---

4. PC(USA), *Book of Common Worship*, 594.
5. PC(USA) and Cumberland Presbyterian Church, *Daily Prayer*, 203.
6. © David B. Batchelder, 2015.

Join us, Lord, at this meal
and gather us in love,
that food and drink and table talk,
will lift our hearts above.

Suggested Prayers for Bedtime

Lord, fill this night with your radiance.
May we sleep in peace and rise with joy,
to welcome the light of a new day in your name.
We ask this through Christ our Lord.[7]

We bless you, God, for the day just spent,
for laughter, tears, and all you've sent.
Grant us, Good Shepherd, through this night,
a peaceful sleep til morning light.
Send angels, Lord, around us here,
to keep our dreaming free from fear.
When morning comes to bring the day,
show us how to follow your way.

Closing Ritual

Session 2 concludes in the manner begun in Session 1: with the passing of water, the sign of the cross, and the words of baptismal remembrance, *"[First Name], remember your baptism and be thankful, you belong to God."* With the opening candlelighting and closing water-signing, these preparation sessions take a shape more worshipful than if the participants gathered for a class or discussion. These sessions are about engagement and encounter, with God and each other. As before, the following prayer, or one similar, is prayed together (copies may be made for all):

---

7. From the antiphon in Keifer, Freburger, and Caulfiel, eds., *Liturgy of the Hours*, 1047. Used by permission of the International Commission on English in the Liturgy. All rights reserved.

SESSION 2: PRAYER AND BAPTISMAL LIFE

God of new beginnings,
from a watery womb
your Spirit birthed us to new life.
Form us in the life of Christ, your Son,
making us faithful as servants
in all you call us;
through Jesus Christ our Lord. **Amen.**

Session 3:
Baptism as a Practiced Way of Life

Opening Ritual

SEE SESSION 1 FOR a description of the common pattern to open a session. This session moves to a deeper consideration of baptismal meaning in relation to scripture.

Reflection on Experience

It is wise for leaders to conduct a kind of check-in with participants, who have hopefully made a beginning with the practice of praying at home. Invite them to share from their experience by asking a few simple questions. Lead anyone who might be so tempted away from thinking in terms of success or failure. If there are some who, for any reason, did not make an attempt, encourage them to do so in the coming week. Since the cultural default for many of us with religion is guilt, leaders must be sensitive to the fragility in parents who are being taken out of their comfort zone to practice something that may likely be outside their personal experience. Adopting an invitational tone to entice and coax participants to share their experience will draw them out and into a conversation that can be affirming. For every attempt to incorporate prayer in the fabric of family is an act of faith and a movement toward God. Here are some suggested questions that might facilitate this sharing.

1. What was your experience at mealtime and bedtime prayer? Describe what happened. What did you notice about yourself and others in your family? What feelings did you have?
2. Which prayer did you use? What drew you to make this choice?
3. What questions or thoughts did your first steps in this practice stir in you?

After a brief period of sharing, leaders can draw the time together by underscoring the connection between prayer and baptismal living. Indeed, the Lord's Prayer itself, often referred to as the prayer of disciples, was part of the instruction given in the ancient church to the unbaptized (those called *catechumens*). The church understood that the life begun in baptism is sustained by the practice of prayer, of which the prayer Jesus taught is the most excellent model. Such use of the Lord's Prayer continues to this day.

Water Stories and a Life of Conversion

In Session 1, the group considered the question, "Why water?" This question is taken up again with the help of additional resources. Printed below is an excerpt from Richard Jespersen's helpful book, *I Am Baptized*. Jespersen offers readers an evocative text useful as a tool for reflection with others on the meaning of baptism. Leaders will want to reproduce this text and have it available for each participant. I suggest having several persons be readers as all follow along with their copy. Because this text is metaphorically dense, readers should be instructed to read slowly. Invite each person to listen for one or two images experienced as particularly compelling. Here is that text:

PART 2: A MODEL OF SACRAMENTAL PREPARATION

Danger!
Baptismal water!
A relentless undertow of grace,
crosscurrents pulling us in over our heads
and out of our depth into Christ;
the drowning of the self-as-god
and the rising of the self-in-Christ.
God buries in a watery grave everything not of God
and raises to new life everything of God,
our watery Good Friday and Easter.

In water
of all shapes and sizes,
in oceans, lakes, rivers, and streams,
in ponds, pools, and puddles,
we go fishing for catch of all kinds, shapes, and sizes.
So also,
in the waters of baptism
we go fishing for people
of all kinds, shapes, and sizes,
God's catch-of-the-day.

To be baptized
is not a solitary experience,
but a family free-for-all.
We are tossed into the water with Jesus
and all who are called to be his disciples,
the whole Christian Church,
in heaven and on earth,
the whole people of God
of all times and places.
To be baptized is to belong!

In water,
we see reflections of the world as it is.
In baptismal water, we see reflections
of the world as it will be,
and we are changed.

SESSION 3: BAPTISM AS A PRACTICED WAY OF LIFE

To live the baptized life
is to follow
the way of the water and Word.
To live baptized
is to walk wet.

You are baptized into this living faith,
the faith of the church
passed by the apostles
through the generations to us,
a great continuum
of baptismal command and promise.

You are baptized,
set afloat
on the great river of God's grace
for the world,
equipped with what has been believed in the church
everywhere
and always
and by everyone.

I, therefore, in faith,
simply receive
what God does
in baptism!
I do not
and cannot add to,
only live in and live out
what God does.
I live by faith in this God who has baptized me!
Affirming my baptism,
I do nothing but simply let be done what is done;
I go with the flow
of God's baptismal doing.
I am baptized!
Amen.
So be it.
Thanks be to God![1]

---

1. Jespersen, *I Am Baptized*, 23, 25, 27, 29, 31, 35, 37.

Having read the text aloud, provide at least a minute of silence before reminding participants of what they are being asked to share. "What images are most striking to you? And, why do you think that is?" Leaders will need to get the feel of the conversation as it unfolds. There is no way to know ahead of time how much response will come from any single question. Sometimes it is helpful to continue nudging the conversation with additional follow-up questions such as, "With which of these images are you 'comfortable' and/or 'uncomfortable?' Why do you think that is?" This line of inquiry opens up the conversation to those aspects of baptism that seem most reassuring and those that appear most challenging, even troubling. What's happening here, of course, is a movement within the conversation into the many layers of meaning having to do with baptism. In a time when the baptism of children in many churches is still laden with sentimentalism, some meanings will bring an element of surprise. The value of this excerpt, therefore, is twofold. Embedded in Jespersen's text are allusions to the Bible's water stories, which illuminate the meaning of the sacrament. Many of these same stories are called forth in the church's baptismal rite, thereby connecting what the church does in baptism with what God has done and continues to do in the world. Second, the language of this text powerfully sets forth Christ's Paschal Mystery, that is, Christ's dying and rising. Though unsettling, the text helps us consider baptism as a life of ongoing conversion, a continual dying to self and being raised in newness with Christ. In a later session, leaders will spend time with participants on the actual service of baptism. In many churches, the act of baptism is accompanied by a series of questions called *renunciations* and *affirmations*, asking those seeking baptism for their child to renounce sin and evil and turn to Jesus Christ and his way of living. These questions themselves bear witness to baptism as a life of ongoing conversation. Thus, the conversation taking place here in Session 3 lays important groundwork for conversations to come later.

SESSION 3: BAPTISM AS A PRACTICED WAY OF LIFE

Diving Deeper

A useful way to transition from Jespersen's text to Scripture is to ask participants, "What meaning do these images suggest of baptism? Can you think of any Bible stories evoked by the images?" It may well be that participants will draw a blank with the second question about Bible stories. That's fine. The purpose of the question is not so much to see what the group knows as it is to establish a curiosity about the fact that baptismal meaning is witnessed to in the water stories of the Bible. These stories include the creation, Noah and the great flood, the passage of the Hebrews through the sea, and Jesus' own baptism. At this point in the conversation, leaders might share the prayer used by the church in its liturgy for baptism. This prayer is referred to by several names: "Thanksgiving for Baptism," "Thanksgiving Over the Water," or "Prayer Over the Water." This prayer is offered by the presiding minister at the time of baptism before that actual act of water pouring or immersing. Its purpose is to give thanks for God's saving acts through water in the past, and it asks that God act now, in baptism, to continue as God has done. Through the prayer, the whole community, with parents and child, remember old stories from a sacred past as God does something marvelous and new in the present.

A close rereading of Jespersen's closing paragraphs helps to bring the conversation to a place of closing. Notice how the text shifts from the third person plural, to the second person, and finally to the first person. What are we to make of this change of voice? Closer consideration makes it clear that the first five paragraphs refer to all of "us" before there is a shift to "you," the one(s) who is(are) to be baptized. Everything affirmed as truth for the community of the baptized becomes, for the ones entering baptismal water, true for them. But the text shifts once more in the last paragraph to the first person so that each reader declares for himself or herself the incredible blessing of baptismal grace: "I, therefore, in faith, simply receive what God does in baptism! I do not and cannot add to, only live in and live out what God does." This statement is where we find ourselves each day all our lives. We are called to live out what God has done. And that living out can be spoken of as learning to "walk wet."

As time allows, leaders may choose to share the following as a way to encourage the practice of prayer in the home. Tertullian was a theologian who lived in the late second century. In his treatise on baptism he wrote, "But we, little fishes, after the example of our [big fish] Jesus Christ, are born in water, nor have-we-safety-in-any-other-way than by permanently abiding in the water."[2] To abide in the water is to walk wet; it is to put our lives before God in trust and dependence for all God desires to do in and through us. Such a life is sustained by prayer. Thus, this conversation has returned to where it began, with a sharing from experience around the practice of prayer in the home. As leaders give new encouragement to establish this practice, participants will have a deeper appreciation for how vital prayer is to living the Christian faith and teaching that faith to their children.

Closing Ritual

Session 3 concludes in the manner begun in the first session. By now, a greater comfort with water, signing, and blessing may be evident. The practice has begun to take root. More than this, a bond has been established. By this session people may be sitting in different places than they were during the first session. This means that they will carry out the ending ritual with others they have now come to know. Something of God has been at work. More than likely, all have begun to sense it. As before, the following prayer, or one similar, is prayed together:

> God of new beginnings,
> from a watery womb
> your Spirit birthed us to new life.
> Form us in the life of Christ, your Son,
> making us faithful as servants
> in all you call us;
> through Jesus Christ our Lord. **Amen.**

---

2. Tertullian, "On Baptism," 669.

Session 4:
Keeping Time in Baptismal Life

Opening Ritual

SEE SESSION 1 FOR a reminder of how to carry out the opening ritual of these preparation sessions. Session 4 extends the conversation concerning family prayer and worship. With the previous discussion of prayer, attention has been given to mealtimes and bedtimes as particularly suitable moments for parents to pray with their children. In this session, the discussion broadens the conversation to consider how the rhythms and seasons of the year, particularly as it is celebrated in the church community, can be a significant aid to family worship. Prior to beginning this subject, however, leaders will want to check in and give participants an opportunity to share from their family experience since the last session.

Calendars and Community

As leaders prepare to lead this session, it will be helpful to think about an important connection to how faith is formed. As parents strive to live their call to form their children's baptismal identity, they need to consider how that identity is impacted by the annual calendar of special days and seasons, including all formal and informal rituals that support it.

We make and keep calendars, and our calendars make and keep us. Keeping time, and how we do it, shapes who we are. For instance, consider the number of times we consult a calendar in any given week; the question is *which* calendar? The answer depends on what it is we're talking about because we have different calendars for work, school, and community activities. We all live with multiple calendars that must be continually referenced and coordinated in order to avoid calendar conflicts that may result in double-booking. For families raising children, calendars become a major intersection of dates, appointments, and activities affecting all members.

Usually a family will keep a calendar tracking all events central to the family's life. With growing children, family calendars become more and more full, eventually bursting with commitments that fill up increasingly busy lives. We can learn a lot about a family by glancing at the family calendar. Calendars reveal the way family life is structured in time around those events which have the highest importance.

The Christian faith has a calendar of its own called the 'liturgical year' that helps God's people remember the past with intentional thankfulness. Keeping this calendar yearly with intentionality also helps us to rehearse the meaning of God for our lives, a meaning that celebrates the blessing of salvation and calls for a fresh commitment to God's purpose in the world. In a word, the liturgical year is central in the life of God's people, because it forms and reforms us in our identity as the baptized community of Christ.

What is true for the church is also true for families in their homes as the domestic church. Remembering and celebrating the significant days and seasons of the year does two important things at once; we express our faith and we are freshly formed *in* that faith. To say it another way, faith's meaning continues to take root in our daily lives in the ways we keep time.

SESSION 4: KEEPING TIME IN BAPTISMAL LIFE

Teaching our children the faith should take account of the natural way keeping time both "forms" and "informs" our lives. The wonderful blessing and privilege we have in starting a family is that we are free to ask ourselves, "What traditions from my upbringing do we want to pass on to the next generation (our children)?" We also want to ask, "What new traditions do we want to begin which we hope will give meaning to our life of faith?" Part of the excitement of growing a family is the sense that we are able to preserve what we treasure from our past, while being free to establish new traditions that add richness and strength to our lives.

This time of preparation for baptism is a splendid opportunity to begin imagining what celebrating the faith at home throughout the year might look like in each family's home. The conversation in Session 4 intends to help this happen. As a way to start the conversation, leaders can invite participants to respond to the following questions: 1) "How many calendars would you say you live by to keep your family on track?" This question is about raising awareness. Though many have shifted to electronic calendars on cell phones and computers, no longer making use of paper calendars, the daily task of keeping track of days and times is just as critical to the way our lives are lived. 2) "Where do you keep a family calendar? What gets written on it? What consequences have you suffered forgetting time (appointments, anniversaries, birthdays, soccer games, etc.)?" These questions will bring to mind the relationship of our calendars to what's most important in our lives. Events we cannot miss, are at least to some degree safeguarded when we have recorded them on a calendar we regularly consult. As this discussion unfolds, it will become more obvious how the practice of keeping calendars is an essential way we share our lives and shape our lives according to our most important priorities. In this sense, calendars reveal our identity, that is, who we are and what our lives are about.

Next, leaders should ask, 3) "What (if anything) comes preprinted when you purchase a calendar? What special days appear automatically on your electronic calendar software?" Here again, these questions intend to raise consciousness. The calendar products we purchase are prepared by merchants who make assumptions about what most of us will want to know about a new year, such as holidays, cultural events, major observances. This is to say that a cultural calendar is already prepared for us with the purchase of a calendar. There really isn't any argument with this. Most of us do not have a problem with this because the culture represented on the calendar is *our* culture; these are days and events important enough to us that we want to remember when they will happen. The point here is that, if the community of the baptized is going to remember particular days and seasons critical for its own identity, it will have to keep its own calendar, and cannot expect public school, civic newsletters, and general society announcements to do it for us.

The question central to this session is what might families, making a commitment in baptism to nurturing their child's faith, do to bring into their homes a celebration of those days and seasons that are central to the Christian community? This is the place where leaders can point to the importance of the church as the faith community to which the families belong. Since the church keeps time according to the liturgical year, families can find helpful ideas from the church's celebrations to bring home and adapt for family use. In addition, families will experience an increasing understanding and enrichment of special days and seasons as they participate regularly in the life of the church over the year. At this point in the conversation, the group is ready for some specific proposals.

Creative Adaptation: Building Faith Traditions in the Home

Many participants will recall family holiday celebrations coinciding with the larger culture that have religious ornamentation. Take Christmas for example: those growing up within a church community may remember a family manger scene with small figures unpacked each season from a shoe box to be set out on a shelf or table. Christmas music, much of it religious in nature, will be familiar because of its omnipresence in public places. And, of course, there is the Christmas tree with decorated branches under which are placed colorfully wrapped presents. Participants may have heard of Advent, the time of waiting before Christmas, which merits little attention from a consumer culture. Some churches invite members into the craft of making an Advent wreath with candles lit as Christmas draws near. These are some of the seasonal activities that have been deposited as customs into our culture. While part of the cultural fabric, they remain largely unconnected to the spiritual meaning from which they first arose. As such, they are part of a religious veneer to which Christianity is a major, but not the sole, contributor. When customs become separated from the meaning that sourced them, they appear quaint and hollowed out. Since the life to which we are born in baptism is a life of deep meaning attuned to God's loving intent for the world, our hunger for meaning leaves us with an ache to know more than we do about such practices. We long for a life where our faith convictions are more clearly expressed in our homes, the place of greatest intimacy with those who are our closest neighbors.

In presenting a child for baptism, parents accept the call to serve as ministers in the ritual life of their family. This not only includes prayer at mealtime and bedtime, but means attending to the days and seasons when the Christian faith is most intensely attentive to what God has done in Jesus Christ. Shaping life in the home for the sake of baptismal living encourages families to revisit their own experience as children having to do with seasonal holidays. It empowers parents to recover the meaning behind the practices they remember. This entails a re-examination of inherited ways of celebrating. Where appropriate, parents may consider revising, adapting, and recreating family rituals so that what is done together more faithfully reflects the spiritual meaning. By being so intentional, parents will give to their children a different set of memories, ones with a stronger rootedness in the meaning behind the doing.

This session introduces a way to begin such reflection and revision. It will need to be supported and strengthened by the church's faith formation ministries over the course of many years. It is worth the effort. Celebrating the liturgical year at home brings the good news of God into our weekday lives, which is the primary place we live out what it means to be baptized.

The preceding reflection is meant to help leaders prepare participants for a conversation to be continued at home. Parents are asked to make time to share together around the following set of questions, taking personal inventory, and coming to some judgements and decisions about how they wish to shape life in their home. 1) "What do you remember about the traditions you grew up with having to do with Christmas and Easter?" 2) "Think about the ways the church keeps liturgical time—the colors, activity, music, words, prayers, and symbols. How might these ways suggest possibilities for your family as you shape your life at home?" 3) "What might it look like for your family to keep Lent, celebrate Pentecost, or give All Saints' Day a place in your home?" Parents should know that this will not be an easy conversation. Leaders realize that Christians are now living in a period where Christianity's dominance over culture is substantially weakening. Churches are having to relearn how to impart to others what could formerly be assumed, given what seemed a predominantly 'Christian' culture. Keen observers are realizing that the Christianity many drew from this culture was less Christian in character than it was cultural in values. So we are all in a place of learning afresh, experimenting, and looking to a more ancient past to give us direction. This baptismal preparation is an expression of that relearning process affecting so much of what the church does.

As this session draws to a close, leaders should provide copies of two examples sharing ideas for how families might celebrate at home. One example pertains to Pentecost and the other to 'Saint Nicholas Day' (December 6). These suggestions are provided below just following the closing prayer for this session. After parents have taken time at home to share with each other around the questions above, they should read these two examples together and imagine possibilities for their family.

SESSION 4: KEEPING TIME IN BAPTISMAL LIFE

Closing Ritual

Session 4 concludes in what has become the practice of these sessions. It is always helpful to take a moment, especially if the conversation has been energetic, to settle minds and hearts before beginning the ritual of water, signing, and blessing. Leaders should not lose sight of how these sessions model for participants how they might make the transition at home to a moment of ritual and prayer. Transitioning is one of the skills we do not give enough thought to as we work to cultivate rituals of worship and prayer in the family. Raising children means living with a mild (or not so mild) level of chaos much of time. Calling the family to dinner and putting children to bed both need the skill of helping others "turn off" their previous activity and "turn on" to the presence of God who is always with us. As before, the following prayer, or one similar, is prayed together:

> God of new beginnings,
> from a watery womb
> your Spirit birthed us to new life.
> Form us in the life of Christ, your Son,
> making us faithful as servants
> in all you call us;
> through Jesus Christ our Lord. **Amen.**

PART 2: A MODEL OF SACRAMENTAL PREPARATION

Planting Seeds for Keeping Pentecost in the Home

Pentecost—A Little Background

Pentecost owes its origins to an agricultural festival of Israel in which the first fruits of the barley harvest were offered to God. Added to this background is the Festival of Booths, in which the Hebrews recalled God's faithfulness in the wilderness as they journeyed from Egypt to the promised land. Each year during this festival, the people would make booths, temporary shelters in which to live for a week in order to remember their heritage. The gift of the Spirit coincides with this feast, enlarging its meaning for Christians. This is the Tower of Babel reversed, the birthday of the church, and beginning of God's new age foreseen by prophets of old. Turn to Luke's wonderful description in the Book of Acts 2:1–21 to read about the 120 disciples praying and waiting together for the promised Spirit, just as Jesus instructed them before his ascension to heaven. Suddenly, the windows shutter open with wind filling the room; tongues of fire appear over the heads of the disciples and all begin praising God in different languages! So amazing was this event that some townsfolk thought they had all gotten drunk with wine. This is a day to be marked by fire, the color red, festivity and surprises, and a warm welcome extended to all.

You Cannot Have Too Much Red!

This day almost demands that we pull out all the stops and go crazy with red: red crepe paper, red balloons, red table cloth, red napkins, red juice as a beverage, red Jell-O, a bowl full of strawberries, even perhaps a shrimp appetizer with red cocktail sauce. Do not underestimate the impact such preparations can have on children when both church and home speak loudly the same truth of God's gift of the Spirit. Naturally, of course, each family member must wear an article of red clothing.

Fire at the Table

Lots of red candles add to the visual imagery of a domestic Pentecost. Several years ago I picked up at a flea market a black metal candelabra capable of holding seven candles. Each year this fifty-cent bargain is brought out for our table to hold seven tall red candles whose flames burn with the fire of Pentecost.

Feasting and Festivity

Pentecost is a day of joyful feasting in God's surprising graciousness. Let your mind run with how this might shape your family's menu for the day and the day's events. Perhaps this might lead you to a barbecue over the grill of some special food that all enjoy. Family games of croquet, badminton, kickball, hide-and-seek, or kite flying are options. Above all, do not treat this day as just another day, or even just another Sunday.

Wind Socks

Hanging strips of red, orange, and yellow ribbon or crepe paper from the blades of ceiling fans (turned on low), or hanging wind socks from tree branches, adds to a sense of the "wind" of the Spirit.

"Gifts of the Spirit" Mobile

A favorite decoration for our family Pentecost is a mobile made of red poster board cut-out flames suspended from twisted coat hanger wire. On each flame is written one of the gifts of the Spirit from Isaiah 11. This is hung near an open window or a screen door, where the breeze keeps it in constant motion. Something as simple as a mobile like this can help children associate the meaning of Pentecost with the Holy Spirit and its presence in their lives at home.

PART 2: A MODEL OF SACRAMENTAL PREPARATION

Hospitality

As Pentecost proclaims the welcome of God for people of every race and nation into one community, so a family's Pentecost might consider this day a day of extending hospitality to others—friends, family, even new persons in the church or neighborhood. What a powerful witness this offers for what God has done to heal divisions and make us one in the Spirit!

A Pentecost Prayer at the Table

God of wind and fire,
send your Spirit upon us here as we share this feast.
Make our hearts burn with love for all your children.
Light up our hearts with gratitude for all your gifts
making us generous with all in need.
Bless us with a boldness to love
so that we, with all the baptized,
may live your justice and peace;
through Jesus Christ our Lord. **Amen.**

Planting Seeds for Saint Nicholas Day, December 6

One Example to Spark the Imagination

Within the season of Advent falls a special date that should not go unobserved: December 6, Saint Nicholas Day, the day when Bishop Nicholas died and was born into God's eternal kingdom. The real-life inspiration for the mythical figure of Santa Claus was a fourth-century bishop with a special concern for children and poor people. Remembering his fabled acts of kindness and generosity can inspire greater faithfulness and can be an opportunity for a moment of abundance in Advent, an otherwise restrained season. Observing Saint Nicholas Day also can help restore the worthwhile origins of our culture's Santa Claus (who has now become almost a symbol for greed and commercialism), as well as provide a foretaste of the Christmas feast to come.

For many years our family has celebrated the Feast of Saint Nicholas. The night before, my wife and I decorate the dining room with candles, hints of Christmas, and the makings of a breakfast feast. We awaken early on the morning of December 6. The table is set with our finest dishes, silverware, teacups, fancy pastries, and fruit rolls. In the center of the table stands a wooden figure of the kindly bishop, which can be purchased at a specialty Christmas store or online.

The purpose of this feast is to remember and celebrate Saint Nicholas's example of compassion for others. Before beginning to eat, each family member draws another member's name from a jar or bowl. On Saint Nicholas Day, we perform secret acts of kindness for the person whose name we have drawn. In this way we seek to be like Bishop Nicholas, who gave generously and secretly. At the end of our meal, we share this prayer:

PART 2: A MODEL OF SACRAMENTAL PREPARATION

God of joy and cheer,
we thank you for your servant, the good bishop Nicholas.
In loving the poor, he showed us your kindness,
in caring for children, he revealed your love.
Make us thoughtful without need of reward
so that we may be good followers of Jesus Christ,
our Savior. **Amen.**

In many places, it is traditional for children to put a pair of shoes outside their bedroom doors on the eve of Saint Nicholas Day. By morning, the shoes are filled with treats. Oranges are traditional delights for this occasion as they remind us how Bishop Nicholas secretly gave a poor father three bags of gold so each of his daughters could fulfill the social norm of the time of having a marriage dowry, and thereby avoid a life of slavery.

Session 5:
Baptismal Life as New Vocation

Opening Ritual

By now, the opening ritual will likely have become normative for the group. This might even be an observation shared by all. It can be helpful for leaders to lift up this observation and comment on ritual's power to shape and form a group when patterns are repeated over time.

Keeping Time Revisited

Leaders will want to hear from participants about their conversations on celebrating liturgical time at home, including their thoughts on suggestions for Pentecost and Saint Nicholas Day. The purpose is not to persuade, but to entice and spark interest in possibilities participants may not have considered. The suggestions that were offered were meant to be "permission giving." Much Christianity in the West is overburdened with words read or spoken. A preponderance of verbiage kills ritual and suffocates festivity because it caters so heavily to the cognitive part of the human brain. Children are best served when words are better balanced with gesture and symbol creatively incorporated into family worship. It is possible that some participants may feel overwhelmed by how much is suggested in what they were asked to read. This should be addressed. These examples reflect what could come about in a gradual building up over years. This is too much for a beginning. Trying to do too much too soon will turn ritual festivity into a burden (one more thing in an already busy life). Time is needed to build new patterns into the home. Begin with a little confidence that the modest changes will make a difference. These reassurances are very important because parents want to do the best for their children, often trying too hard, doing too much. There must be joy. So, rather than hearing these or any ideas in the imperative (i.e., you must), it is much better to help parents feel both empowered and trusted with the stewardship of their families, and eager to take a few well-chosen steps of building a new faith tradition that can make a difference.

Being "Called" in Baptism

In this part of the session, leaders will need to have arranged a small table with a variety of objects such as a towel, hammer, hairbrush, toothbrush, screwdriver, table utensils, scissors, kitchen knife, cell phone, remote control, sewing needle, butane candle lighter, etc. (Be sure to cover these objects until you are ready to begin this part of the session.) These suggested objects share something relevant to this conversation. Leaders can ask participants what these objects share in common. The answer is almost too obvious. All are useful but each one requires some instruction before it can be of value. Imagine, then, how an inability to make use of these objects would put life under limitation. The point of this little exercise is to make plain an important insight without merely telling it. This insight is meant to help all to see how much "living the faith" is dependent on *skills* we learn. Just as life as human beings involves acquiring necessary skills not innately given at birth, so baptismal life requires skills that we learn through instruction and practice over time. Leaders will want to ask participants, "What faith *skills* can you think of that are necessary to living the faith?" As participants share, the leader may write them down on a chalkboard, newsprint, or invite all to jot them down. Among those likely to be named are: learning to pray, reading the Bible, worship, singing hymns, caring for others—these all have a skill base not to be overlooked. Next, leaders should ask, "What would you pick as the top three items you will teach your child how to use and why? What spiritual skills do you think your child will need most and why?" A case can be made that all are equally important. The point is not to rank them but to create a conversation in which participants consider the important of each. The leader can now draw this stage of the conversation to a close by saying, "What we promise God at the baptism of our children is that we, as parents and as a faith community, will undertake this spiritual training with them."

In the Presbyterian rite of baptism, parents make promises to equip their children with spiritual skills that will serve them throughout their lives. They are asked to respond to the following question: *Relying on God's grace, do you promise to live the Christian faith, and to teach that faith to your child?* The question does not spell out what this "teaching" means, what it looks like, or consists of. It is a general reference to spiritual practices essential for any human being to live out the new life given by God in baptism. Since the Christian faith is more caught than taught, it is helpful to return to Mark Searle's insight from Session 2, that we do not so much promise to teach our children *merely what we know*, as much as we promise to learn anew the story *with them*. This idea of learning anew the Christian story with our children has a strong appeal because we need not be experts, only fellow seekers. Moreover, we are not alone in this. Our lives are all lived in relationship within a faith community. What this connection means can be imagined with the following language: *it is a shared journey, as fellow pilgrims, worshiping together, in the company of the saints, serving neighbors in need.*

Notice that the emphasis of this statement rests heavily on the *communal* nature of baptismal living. The life we are given is a shared life. It cannot be lived in isolation. While our formation in faith happens in the human body given us by God, we participate in the spiritual body of Christ's many-membered church. The

PART 2: A MODEL OF SACRAMENTAL PREPARATION

Christian faith has always had an abiding *we*-ness. This means that the skills and practices parents learn and teach their children are found alive and active in the faith community to which they belong. As every baptismal liturgy proclaims, baptism makes us members of Christ's body, and growing into our baptismal identity happens *within* this community.

Leaders are now ready to ask participants about four words and how they are related: *community, faith, forming, in*. Ask the group how it would put them together. Seven combinations are possible, each one intriguing to consider:

1. Forming faith in community
2. Forming community in faith
3. In community forming faith
4. Faith in forming community
5. Faith forming in community
6. Community in forming faith
7. In faith forming community

Leaders will need to have these printed out to distribute to all in the session. Ask participants, "Which arrangement speaks most strongly to you? What do they share in common?" People may find it difficult to choose one over the others. Each statement nuances a different aspect of a larger meaning. No one statement is complete by itself. Each offers a way to think about what it means to belong to a community that is not quite captured by another. Together, they help us look at the importance of community from all sides, helping us appreciate the critical role of living baptism in community. Moreover, these statements help us see more clearly how faith finds its home in community even as community is *constantly reshaped* by the faith that forms it.

SESSION 5: BAPTISMAL LIFE AS NEW VOCATION

Who Helped Shaped You?

Having come to realize the importance of the community to parents' responsibility to teach their children the faith, leaders are ready to ask, "Is there a person you can identify whose life (in a particular way) shaped you in your relationship with God? Who was it, how old were you, and how did it happen?" These questions invite participants to see from their own experience the importance other people have had helping form their faith. Some may identify a person whose influence came when they were quite young. Parents are now in a position to make something important available to their children. In these or similar words, leaders should share the following: "One gift you can give your child is the treasured memory of special Christian people who embrace them with Christ's love. Bringing your child into the company of the saints each Sunday, from birth onward, makes possible for her or him the making of memories rooted in the deepest regions of heart, mind, and soul. Your attention to the *we*-ness of baptismal living can give your child the chance to form profound relationships with others that will form and inform your child's life with God."

It is always wise for leaders to encourage ways for participants to *take the conversation home to be continued*. Thoughtfully consider those in your church who have turned a kindly face, spoken a friendly word, and shown sincere interest in you and your child. Parents should be encouraged to consider how they might grow these relationships as time and circumstance affords. It may be that the relationships formed in these preparation sessions provide a beginning. Commonly, churches that provide a Sunday nursery have it staffed by caregivers of a saintly disposition whose love for children mirrors the love of Christ, the Good Shepherd. This ministry of the church is an excellent place for parents to begin the bond of Christian love between their child and another member of the church.

PART 2: A MODEL OF SACRAMENTAL PREPARATION

Closing Ritual

As with the previous sessions, Session 5 concludes with the ritual of water, signing, and blessing. By this point in the preparation process, participants should have a deeper appreciation for the significance of forming relationships within the community. Indeed, that awareness should include those with whom they have shared in these sessions. Being mindful of such relatedness will intensify the closing ritual with a deepened sense of thanksgiving. Indeed, the place to which the group has arrived in this session reflects a journey filled with rich and unexpected blessings. As before, the following prayer, or one similar, is prayed together:

> God of new beginnings,
> from a watery womb
> your Spirit birthed us to new life.
> Form us in the life of Christ, your Son,
> making us faithful as servants
> in all you call us;
> through Jesus Christ our Lord. **Amen.**

Session 6:
Full Initiation—Water, Oil, Bread, and Wine

Opening Ritual

By this session, leaders will be able to observe how natural the opening ritual centers the group, helping it to focus its attention for the sake of the conversation to come.

Baptismal Dignity and a
Welcome to the Table

Session 6 invites participants to consider how the water bath of baptism and holy meal of the Lord's Supper are inseparably connected, not only theologically, but experientially. To open up the senses and imagination to this conversation, leaders will need to prepare a table on which the following objects are placed: fork and steak knife, cloth napkin, burp cloth, baby bottle, plastic sippy cup, wine glass, coffee mug, baby bib, and dinner plate. The table may be available for viewing as people arrive at the session or the table may be covered with a cloth. Give participants a few brief moments to examine the objects with the help of a question: "As you look over these objects, what thoughts run through your mind with respect to your child?"

This question is fairly wide open, and is meant to be so. Participants will recognize that these items all pertain to meals. Someone may note that there is a degree of differentiation according to age and capacity. But there is another insight more central to the purpose of this conversation, and the leader must be sure to make this point. Whatever age we may be thinking about, life must be fed in order for it to live and thrive. Consider that a child's inability to make use of utensils does not pose a barrier to eating and drinking. We do not postpone eating until such skill is acquired; we accommodate to the level of personal development. This is also true of baptismal life and its need for nourishment, in particular, the nourishment we receive from communing at the Lord's Supper. Just as it is true in our homes, we do not expect adult levels of competence and social skill from our children before we permit them to sit at the table and dine with the family. Parents know that their child's capacity grows through the experience of being with them at the meal, as parents and older siblings guide appropriately at each stage of development. Foremost in children's meal-taking formation is their presence and participation with the whole family at an unsegregated table. So it is with the newly baptized, and the meal that sustains that life we call the Lord's Supper, Holy Communion, or Eucharist.

This conversation seeks to open parent's minds and imaginations to how they might nurture their children in the faith through their full participation in the liturgy of Word and sacrament. Such participation includes a parent bringing her or his child to the holy meal from baptism on. In the Rite of Baptism for the Evangelical Lutheran Church in America, there is a beautiful passage spoken by the presiding minister to the parents of the child being baptized. The words anticipate many years in which the spiritual care of the child will rest upon parents' initiative. In particular, the statement sets forth the child's full participation in the liturgy as central to baptismal formation. It also calls parents to help their child grow into the baptismal call to serve the needy. Session 6 is an excellent time for participants to hear this text read.

SESSION 6: FULL INITIATION—WATER, OIL, BREAD, AND WINE

> As you present your daughter/son for baptism,
> you are entrusted with gifts and responsibilities:
> to live with her/him among God's faithful people,
> bring her/him to the word of God *and the holy supper*,
> and nurture her/him in faith and prayer,
> so that she/he may learn to trust God,
> proclaim Christ through word and deed,
> care for others and the world God made,
> and work for justice and peace among all people.[1]

This statement deserves some time so it can be unpacked. Notice the statement's structure—how living "among God's people," bringing the child "to the word of God and the holy supper," as well as "nurture" in faith and prayer all contribute to a vital purpose. Line six begins, "so that," indicating that parental attentiveness to the above named are for the purpose of learning trust, proclaiming Christ, caring for the world and others, and working for justice and peace. The act of baptism is the beginning of a special vocation into which we are formed over a lifetime. Leaders might ask participants to identify a particular line in the statement that most captures their attention. After a brief discussion, leaders should call participants to return to line four. Session 6 provides a conversation on the essential relationship between baptism and Eucharist for vitality of faith, and the flowering of trust and service. Full initiation into the Christian faith presumes not only baptism, but also includes coming to the Table to be fed, in bread and wine, the same Christ with whom we are joined in the waters of the font. "In baptism the eucharist begins and in the eucharist baptism is sustained."[2]

One of the tragic developments in the history of the church was an inadequate understanding of the relationship between baptism and the Lord's Supper. One result still lingering in sacramental practice has been for churches to postpone the participation of baptized children in the Lord's Supper until they are considered old enough to understand its meaning. Thankfully, this distorted

---

1. ELCA, *Evangelical Lutheran Worship*, 584. Adapted slightly; italics added.
2. Kavanagh, *Shape of Baptism*, 122.

practice is being reformed in many denominations. This process of baptismal preparation presented in this book invites participants into a renewal of diminished sacramental practice so that every child baptized is welcomed on that same day (and every Sunday thereafter) to the Lord's Supper. As participants have discovered throughout these preparation sessions, the faith of children is formed from birth, recognizing that a child's capacity for God is a gift that must be nurtured. Being made to share Christ's life in baptism, children need the grace given in the meal where Christ continues to give himself for our weakness. This need is no less felt by a child because their cognitive powers have yet to mature. "Children experience much that they cannot verbally articulate. We do not delay the first bath until the child understands hygiene, nor do we require knowledge of nutrition prior to the first meal."[3] There is no environment so sensorially rich as the liturgy for the Lord's Day, where all God's people come to hear and say, taste and see, gesture and bless in the fullness of grace, meeting us where we are to form us in what we are called to be. In the liturgy, children learn what cannot be taught.[4]

Some years ago, Presbyterians were seeking how to respond to questions from churches having to do with the relationship between baptism and the Lord's Supper. Some questioned whether baptism was necessary to one's participation at the Holy Table. Others were raising questions born from a casual baptismal practice referred to as "indiscriminate baptism,"[5] that is, baptizing "on demand" without consideration of how those initiated might be formed in the faith over time. Questions were also raised about whether anything of God really happens at the font, believing that baptism was really a time of witness to a personal confession of faith. Confusion of this nature regarding the sacraments remains with us today, and calls for careful conversation and renewed liturgical practice. To this end, Presbyterians formed a study group that produced a document titled *Invitation to Christ*, which provides

3. Weil, "Children and Worship," 59.
4. Kavanagh, *Elements of Rite*, 16.
5. Byars, "Indiscriminate Baptism and Baptismal Integrity," 36–40.

SESSION 6: FULL INITIATION—WATER, OIL, BREAD, AND WINE

helpful background and theology as well as calling for changes in the liturgy. One part of the document is relevant to Session 6:

> At Eucharist we are fed and nourished to live the baptismal life. The Christ with whom we are joined in baptism, and whose body we are, continues to give himself to us in the meal that bears his name. As the only repeatable part of Christian initiation, the Lord's Supper draws us more deeply into the paschal mystery of our dying and rising with Christ.[6]

One of the key insights of this document is how changed liturgical experience leads to deepened understanding; that is, we are formed from the inside out. Our minds come to think differently as our bodies persuade us because of new experience. Session 6 encourages such learning for participants, as well as the church itself.

Leaders are asked to follow the wisdom of the preceding discussion and prepare participants for an experience of full initiation when their children are baptized. This will mean communing the children at the Lord's Supper in the same service as they are baptized. Some explanation will be necessary. I suggest the following: tell participants to sit somewhere near the front of the church and not to worry if their child makes the typical sounds one would expect. The hospitality of the assembly does not expect absolute silence. The coos or cries of a child are joyous to the ears of those who are advancing in age. Should a child's discomfort rise to a level of distress, parents should know they are free at any point in the service to leave and return without fear of disruption. (See the following conversation regarding congregational hospitality to children.) At the time when the people are to be communed, the presiding minister should invite the newly baptized and their families to come forward first. If the newly baptized infant is brought forward for Communion, the presider may dip a finger in the chalice and place a very small amount of wine on the inside of the child's lips. For children of a slightly older age, a small piece of bread may be given. Communing in this way is simple, dignified,

---

6. PC(USA), *Invitation to Christ*, 30.

intimate, and powerfully meaningful to the whole assembly of the inseparable relationship between the sacraments.

For further reflection on this connection, leaders may hand out a sheet on which is printed the statements provided below.

- "Admission to the Sacrament is by invitation of the Lord, presented through the Church to those who are baptized."[7]
- "Infants and children may be communed for the first time during the service in which they are baptized or they may be brought to the altar during communion to receive a blessing."[8]
- "The invitation to the Lord's Supper is extended to all who have been baptized, remembering that access to the Table is not a right conferred upon the worthy, but a privilege given to the undeserving who come in faith, repentance, and love."[9]
- "Baptized children who are being nurtured and instructed in the significance of the invitation to the Table and the meaning of their response are invited to receive the Lord's Supper, recognizing that their understanding of participation will vary according to their maturity."[10]

Wisdom and Beatitude: Formed in Worship

It has been clear throughout this process that families should be encouraged to participate together in the liturgy for the Lord's Day. There is a role for the church nursery, but it is not as a holding station until children are considered old enough according to adult expectations of being able to sit still and quietly listen. The nursery is part of the church's formation ministry, helping families ease their children over time into full participation. Like everyone else, some days will flow more easily and others will not. Alternative

---

7. ELCA, *Use of the Means of Grace*, 41.
8. Ibid., 42.
9 PC(USA), *Book of Order*, W-2.4011a, p. 98.
10. Ibid., W-2.4011b, p. 98.

programs, some of them quite fine in themselves, can never take the place of children's actual participation in the liturgy itself. Such participation is formational because it is a learning *by* doing *with* others, and watching others, especially other family members, who *model* for the child. Therefore, children should be encouraged to participate in worship from the day of their baptism, making such allowances as are appropriate and needed.

Leaders should have a conversation, however briefly, on the role of parents and the congregation at large in the hospitality provided children in worship. For many years, West Plano Presbyterian Church has been thoughtful about this responsibility and has been intentional about becoming a community of welcome. There have been growing pains along the way, but this has not deterred this church from its determination to become a formational community for those of all ages.

The following resource[11] was developed to help serve this purpose. It is based on the five core values: (1) wisdom and beatitude; (2) baptismal "dignity" of all; (3) mutual love and forbearance; (4) readiness to participate is a process of growth; and (5) community boundaries are a caring expression of love for all. As an example of what one church has done, this resource may be a conversation starter among leaders or between leaders and those responsible for the care and nurture of children in worship.

Living Our Baptismal Vows in the Liturgy: Faithful Formation of Children in Worship

> BLESSED is the church whose children are welcomed into the fullness of the church's sacramental liturgy, for they—over time and with patience—shall know their identity and calling as disciples of the Risen Lord.
>
> WISE is the church that partners with parents in making nurturing space and providing guidance for all, especially the youngest among us.

---

11. Prepared by the leadership of Worship & Music, Formation for Discipleship and staff of West Plano Presbyterian Church. © WPPC, June 2011.

PART 2: A MODEL OF SACRAMENTAL PREPARATION

The language of blessing and wisdom borrows from the rich tradition of Scripture in calling the church to the wonder and delight of formation *in and for* the liturgy. This blessing and wisdom serves to guide our relationship with one another as we gather each Lord's Day for worship.

Therefore, blessed and wise are adults, parents, and children who practice reciprocity of hospitality and care. The reflections and guidance are grounded on this principle.

Basic Guidance

For Parents

Actively prepare your child at home for worship by "practicing" and discussing behaviors necessary for full *and* reverent participation with others in worship where there are fewer individual liberties. During worship:

- Lovingly instruct (form) your child to be considerate of others by helping him/her engage appropriately in the liturgy.

- Resist the temptation to "entertain" your child in worship because this may have unintended consequences requiring the unlearning of bad habits.

- Attend to your child's demonstrated personal needs. Extend hospitality to her/him by providing relief from part or all of the liturgy as needed.

- Make use of the nursery, for part or all of the liturgy, to support your child's ongoing formation in worship participation.

- Provide, when necessary, "quiet" books or toys to complement your child's participation in worship.

For the Assembly

Worship is communion with God *and* communion with God's people of all ages. During worship:

SESSION 6: FULL INITIATION—WATER, OIL, BREAD, AND WINE

- Treat children and adults alike as your sisters and brothers in Christ. We all share a common baptismal identity and, therefore, all should show one another mutual respect and dignity.

- Leave "parenting" to parents. When you witness a parent tending a restless child, show understanding, patience, and love as you return your focus to worshiping God.

- Bear any personal inconvenience with love.

- Never underestimate anyone's capacity, including a child's, to experience God. We cannot presume to know the degree to which a child is apprehending the holy.

Reflections for Parents in the Assembly

Blessed are we for the gifts children bring us of openness, wonder, joy, and surprise without which we would be poorer.

Wise, therefore, are parents who prepare their children for worship by actively helping them develop behaviors appropriate for worship:

- to be respectful of others in the worship space,

- to sing the alleluias and to keep the silences,

- to share the peace and to receive the sacraments.

Blessed are the children whose parents nurture in them a reverence for the holy encountered in each liturgy.

Wise are parents who know that learning *discipleship* involves *discipline* and, therefore, gently exercise discipline for the sake of their child's faith formation.

Blessed is the child who is not made the center of attention in worship and discovers the priceless joy of a mind, heart, and body centered on the triune God.

Wise are parents who recognize that ways of attending to children in other settings may be inappropriate in worship.

Reflections for Others in the Assembly

Blessed is the congregation that welcomes and affirms the special gifts that children bring to the whole assembly.

Wise, therefore, are we when we honor children and parents by remembering:

- to model full and attentive participation in the liturgy,
- to refrain from actions that stimulate a child,
- to lovingly engage children at appropriate times in the liturgy.

Blessed is the congregation that practices patience and love, remembering Jesus' words when he said, "whoever welcomes a child in my name welcomes me."

Wise are we when we welcome children as bearers of unsolicited grace and mercy.

Blessed are children when the church communicates God's unconditional love.

Wise is the church that sees in its children not only the future, but the present.

The Shape of the Baptismal Rite

There remains the practical matter of attending to baptismal rite itself, with such questions as when to move, where to stand, how to answer the ritual questions, the role of sponsors or godparents, etc. The close of Session 6 may be such a time. Or, leaders may need to arrange a separate time with the presiding minister to cover these details. For this session, it will be necessary for leaders to have a copy of, and be familiar with, the baptismal rite used by their congregation. The common shape of baptism as formed in the ecumenical consensus is as follows:

Presentation

Introduction—No one image can speak the fullness of baptism's mystery. Baptism is new birth, death and dying, incorporation, being washed in Christ, and so much more!

Presentation—No one comes to God on her/his own but by God's grace acting through others.

Profession

Renunciation of Evil—The way we enact baptism is a parable for the life of faith. Each day we continue to grow up into our baptism. It is an ongoing, lifelong conversion from sin and evil to the holiness and love of God.

Profession of Faith—Our faith is joined to the faith of the church, which is faith in the triune God. Together we profess our confidence that what God has done in Christ is mediated to us through the Holy Spirit.

Baptism

Thanksgiving Over the Water—We praise God for God's saving deeds through water.

Baptism—Acting through the church, God bestows new life.

Laying On of Hands—Life in Christ is life empowered by the Holy Spirit.

Signing of the Cross—With oil, the candidate is marked with the cross of Christ.

PART 2: A MODEL OF SACRAMENTAL PREPARATION

Welcome

Presentation of Candle—Born anew, we are called to bear Christ's light in the world.

Welcome—God adds to our number, the church rejoices, and embraces the newly baptized.

The Peace—As sisters and brothers in Christ, we share Christ's gift of peace.

Lord's Supper—The newly baptized is communed for the first time.

Even if it is necessary to schedule a "walk-through" at another time, there is value in the group relocating itself to the worship space for the closing of this session. More specifically, assembling at the baptismal font can be a way of recapitulating the whole of the preparation process. Throughout these sessions, the preparation process was imagined as "walking wet," and as a "shared journey, as fellow pilgrims, worshiping together, in the company of the saints, serving neighbors in need." It will mean something to the participants for them to consider that when they next gather together, it will be in the space they now stand, beside baptismal water, and in the company of those who will welcome the children of these parents as new sisters and brothers in Christ.

Closing Ritual

In each of the previous sessions, a bowl of water was passed from person to person as a water cross was traced on each one, and words of affirmation and blessing were spoken. Now the participants will be asked to move to the baptismal font to dip their thumb in the water for the sign of the cross. If the font is empty, the leader will need to make provision for water to be poured from a pitcher or ewer at the time of this closing. There are subtle but meaningful connections to be made between this final ritual and those the group has experienced in previous sessions. What remains the

SESSION 6: FULL INITIATION—WATER, OIL, BREAD, AND WINE

same—the water, signing, and words—is now moved into a larger communal space. It is a space these parents have entered before, perhaps many times. Now they do so with a fullness of thanksgiving, richer understanding, and heightened expectation. They are not the same as they were before Session 1. Something has happened in each one, though it may elude them as to what it is precisely. However God's Spirit has worked throughout this process, it likely includes a deepening sense of each person's own baptism, what it means to be so gifted and called. This is as it should be, for "Remember your baptism and be thankful, you belong to God." Each will hear this said with his or her name, and each will speak it over another. When the tracing of a cross on each is completed, the prayer may be offered by the leader or spoken by all.

> God of new beginnings,
> from a watery womb
> your Spirit birthed us to new life.
> Form us in the life of Christ, your Son,
> making us faithful as servants
> in all you call us;
> through Jesus Christ our Lord. **Amen.**

Assessing Pastoral Challenges and Opportunities

To embark on such a ministry as I have here proposed constitutes an intervention. It is to cut a new path outside the experience of most in our churches. For pastors, it will likely call for a willingness to reassess current theological understandings of sacramental practice, and to learn new skills not taught in seminary. We should not be daunted. All of us are living in a time of overall reassessment in light of new understandings of faith and formation, a new ecumenical consensus challenging denominational "enclave theology,"[1] and a keener grasp of major cultural shifts affecting the relationship between religion and culture. Coinciding with these changes is a recovery of baptismal identity that engages us in lifelong, ongoing conversion to the Christ who claims us, calls us, and is with us always, to the end of the age.

Those churches and leaders interested in this book's proposal will need to navigate a number of pastoral hurdles on which I would like to briefly comment.

---

1. See Hunsinger, *Eucharist and Ecumenism*, 1, who writes: "By 'enclave' theology, I mean a theology based narrowly in a single tradition that seeks not to learn from other traditions and to enrich them, but instead to topple and defeat them, or at least to withstand them. Enclave theology is polemical theology even when it assumes an irenic facade. Its limited agenda makes it difficult for it to take other traditions seriously and deal with them fairly. . . . Enclave theology makes itself look good, at least in its own eyes, by making others look bad."

ASSESSING PASTORAL CHALLENGES AND OPPORTUNITIES

1. *Breaking old patterns and setting new norms take work.*

Every church that baptizes infants already has a way it goes about baptizing children. Whatever that way is and however faithful it may be judged, it is what many expect from the church. To introduce something new to the process requires ministers to get out in front and begin shaping new expectations that better cohere with the theological vision offered in this book. It will not be helpful to wait until parents telephone the minister to request baptism before introducing the idea of a period of baptismal preparation. Grandparents may already have booked airline passage, the christening gown may be hanging in the closet, and invitations to a postbaptism celebration may be ready to drop in the mail. Trying to make a change in the face of already formed plans such as these is like trying to swim up a waterfall. Wise leaders will need to bring existing committee or ministry team structures onboard and gain their support. Avoiding the language of "requirement" is critical. The church must not be seen as regulating grace; the church offers experiences filled with grace that are intended to be received as gifts. How language is couched is not a mere matter of semantics. Our use of language can reframe ministry so that people engage opportunities with open hearts and minds. Some years ago, West Plano Presbyterian Church wrote a communication brochure for its website to be made available wherever and whenever it seemed wise to do so (for example, when a pregnancy was announced). What follows is the text of that brochure. It is meant to be an example of how one church sought to speak in terms of gift, rather than regulation.

The Church's Care for Parents on the Occasion of a Child's Birth[2]

Congratulations on the birth of your child!

The congregation of West Plano Presbyterian Church rejoices with you. We are ready to support and encourage

2. Copyright © West Plano Presbyterian Church, November 17, 2004.

you as you begin the exciting and challenging journey of parenting.

As parents of a new child, we know that the years ahead will be filled with much blessing as well as times of struggle. Yet, we are not alone. God is with us, especially in the form of a faith community that surrounds us with love and care. Our church wants to be such a community for you.

Questions that might appear in the future

The information in this brochure has been prepared to help you understand better the form which this love and care takes, especially as you might have questions about Christian baptism and church programs to help families to grow in faith.

So much joy, we want to express it!

Parents are filled with excitement when a new child is born. The long nine-month wait is full with hope and some anxiety. At our child's birth, our hearts are overwhelmed with gratitude for what God has given us. Our faith in God may lead us to wonder, how can we say thanks?

A way to give thanks

The first ministry, which the church offers new parents, is a brief rite (a rite is a short service) called "Thanksgiving for the Gift of a Child."[3] This rite takes place in a Sunday morning worship service. It gives parents, family members, and the congregation an opportunity to say "thank you" to God and to ask God's blessing upon both child and parents as they begin their family life. This opportunity may take place on almost any Sunday when scheduling permits.

---

3. For examples of such rites, see Archbishop's Council, *Common Worship* (2000); Episcopal Church, *Book of Occasional Services, 1994*; and Church of Scotland, *Welcome to a Child*, 1–23.

Assessing Pastoral Challenges and Opportunities

Thinking about Christian baptism and wondering what to do about it

Baptizing infants is not something every denomination practices. Presbyterians practice infant baptism for member parents when the parents are *ready* to receive the gift of baptism and accept the responsibilities that baptism asks of us. What this means is that parents never need to panic if their baby is not baptized before reaching a certain age. Presbyterians do not believe that unbaptized infants are in danger, because they are held in God's love from birth. At the same time, there is no need for parents to put baptism off until their child grows older when an individual decision can be made. Presbyterians believe that baptism is the gift *of* faith, not a reward *for* faith. Thus, as we have said, the time is right for baptism when parents are *ready* to "receive the gift and accept the responsibility."

What does this mean?

In baptism, a child begins new life in Christ, which is filled with promise and potential. Since baptism begins, rather than completes, the Christian life, growing up in Christ is a necessary part of being baptized. This is why baptism in the Presbyterian church asks parents to commit themselves to "live the Christian faith and teach that faith to their child." Presbyterian baptism expects that parents will be active in their child's faith development, coming together to church and nurturing their child in the way of Jesus Christ.

How will we know how to help our child grow in faith?

Helping parents "get ready" for baptism is a responsibility required of every Presbyterian church. "It takes a village to raise a child" is an expression that fits perfectly with the church. Parents are never alone in their role of forming children in the faith. At the same time, the church cannot nurture faith without parents taking their responsibility. So the church and parents form a partnership to do this wonderful work together. This is something we take time to talk about as we look ahead to baptism.

> So how do we get moving toward
> the baptism of my child?

It begins with parents themselves, taking time to talk together and come to a decision. Do you remember our earlier remark about parents being ready to "receive the gift and accept the responsibility"? Readiness for baptism is something the church never pushes on parents but always invites parents into. It is different for different families. Some parents are ready soon after their child's birth and others want to take more time to let thing settle down before deciding to walk the path to baptism. Why is this the case? It is simply due to the fact that no two families are the same. We come from different backgrounds and our personal circumstances are varied. So deciding when to begin the path to baptism is first up to the parents. Usually, a sign of parent readiness is when parents begin again attending worship and involving themselves in the life of the church. The reason this is a sign of readiness is because baptism itself asks us to commit ourselves to participate in the life of the church.

> I think I am ready to walk the path
> to baptism, so what's next?

When parents are ready to begin they should contact the church and its pastor so that the church can welcome them into the process of preparation for baptism. This welcome takes place on a Sunday morning in worship and marks the start of the process. Since baptism is about more than just the family but affects the whole church, it is fitting that we all join hands in this process of preparing for baptism.

What does this process look like?

The process involves a series of discussions and sharing around what it means to receive the gift of baptism and live the responsibilities that baptism involves. In baptism, parents and congregation make promises, so it is important that we spend time understanding what these promises mean and how they can be incorporated into our everyday lives. In this process we share ideas, ask questions, learn from one another, and explore helpful faith resources that will strengthen a family in its faith at home. Also, it is important that we get to know one another better since nurturing a child in the faith is something we do over years rather than in months.

How long does this preparation for baptism take?

Usually, this preparation period extends over a few months in six to eight meetings that take place on Sundays. As best we can, we design a schedule that will try to fit each family's circumstances. Wherever possible, we like to bring more than one family together in this process, but this cannot always be the case. This preparation for baptism is led by our church staff and dedicated church members who share in this ministry.

When do we set the date of baptism?

Early in the preparation process we will look at the church calendar and consider the best available times for baptism. The church calendar has built into it special baptismal festival days and seasons, which are the most desirable times for baptism. These times are rich with meaning and have a long history associated with baptism. We always make sure that the date for baptism is set far enough in advance so that special guests will have time to be present if so desired.

A final word and prayer

This church takes seriously our responsibility to you. We want to give you the best care and nurture as you

PART 2: A MODEL OF SACRAMENTAL PREPARATION

begin parenthood. What we describe in this brochure offers this kind of loving care. It may be that you are unused to such an involved preparation for baptism as we offer here.

We hope you will see how much of our lives and faith we want to share with you. We also hope that you will recognize that baptism should never be a quick decision but something considered after thinking and praying about how it affects our whole lives. When parents have approached baptism in this way, they have discovered a deep renewal of faith, a bonding with the church family, and new strength to raise their children in the way of Jesus Christ. We hope to hear from you soon. May God guide and direct you as consider your decision to begin this process.

2. *Trust experience to persuade, rather than arguments to convince.*

People cannot be debated into changing their minds. Instead, when change happens, what is discovered is that experience has played a key, or even decisive role. Moving to a more intentional ministry of preparation for baptism can generate resistance, particularly when it collides with primary considerations of personal convenience. Many Protestant churches with liturgical roots have not, in practice, lived by that inheritance, which includes taking more thoughtful account of the timing of baptism and communal dimensions of baptism. Instead, more often than not, baptism is scheduled when all the primary actors (parents, extended family, and preferred minister) can coordinate their schedules. Little weight is given in decision making to the fact that the church has had a long tradition of baptismal festival days (All Saints, Baptism of the Lord, Easter, and Pentecost). Moreover, the significance of the relationship between the family of the baptized and the community sharing responsibility for the child's ongoing nurture is secondary to the familial aspects of the ritual as it is so often celebrated. What this means is that leaders will need to exercise patience and formulate an inviting, even enticing appeal to families seeking baptism so that the experience of these preparation sessions can do its work of changing perspective.

3. *Always keep in mind that messiness in ministry is the new condition of the church.*

There was once a time, still in living memory, when the church's ministry entailed choosing, instituting, and maintaining programs. To hear such language sounds archaic in light of the wilderness in which we now find ourselves. For those looking, an abundance of prepackaged ministry models exist, each with well-known names offering endorsements. However, we must now contend with conditions not faced (or at least to the same degree) just a few decades ago. These conditions include aging congregations, insider anxiety, outsider suspicion, a younger generation alert to hypocrisy, opposition to change in some, and change for change's sake in others. In the midst of such conditions, people become defensive, develop unrealistic expectations, turn to finger-pointing, become cautious then careless (or careless then cautious), all resulting much too often in decisions based more on pragmatism than theology. Under such conditions, the church cannot become its most faithful self.

It is always fascinating to see how often the writers of the epistles make an appeal for self-examination and self-awareness. For example, Paul's admonitions in Galatians 6 presume just this kind of self-reflection. To paraphrase, with some homiletical license, Paul says:

> Be gentle when helping those who have wandered off the path, but be careful that you do not stray off course. Bear each other's burdens as Christ would have us, but don't make yourself a burden by expecting others to do everything for you. As important as you are to God, you are never as important as you think you are, so test the quality of your own work. Avoid comparing yourself with your neighbor; it will either feed your pride or stoke your envy. Don't act stupidly and think God doesn't notice. We reap what we sow.

There would be no point for Paul to counsel as he does were it not that being the church in its life and ministry is messy. According to Paul, the only way to fruitfully engage life in community without a personal meltdown is to embrace the cross, which calls us again and again to die to self and be raised with Christ. Paul's expression "crucified to the world" alludes to the meaning of baptism, through which every member of the community is joined to the crucified and risen Lord. This dying to self is the basis for self-reflection, out of which community members can reconsider previous responses by asking themselves what it would mean for them, in this moment of time and space, to say yes to the cross.

Attending to an intentional process of preparation for baptism will, over time, enlarge baptism in the community's spiritual consciousness. That consciousness will grow, and it will slowly take in everything the church is and does. People will make connections. They will start getting it, even speaking about it with a new vocabulary that has meaning and gives power to their lives. Since we become members of Christ's body through baptism, there is nothing the church does that is not *out of* its baptismal identity. Everything *lived out* and *expressed from* the church's life is born from the water of baptism. So, it can be said, the church's ministry entails a calling people to and preparing them for baptism. And, its ministry is also living out our baptism, working for justice, mercy, and peace.

Baptism is the *meta-metaphor* that brings coherence to all the church is, all it says, all it does.

4. *Seeking out kindred spirits and inviting them to learn with you is indispensable.*

The well-being of the church in relation to preparation for baptism will best be served when the minister or key leader identifies several others with whom to nurture this ministry. Readers will want to revisit Part 1 of this book and review the matters of primary concern. These will help formulate in the imagination the qualities, gifts, experience, and skills to look for in possible ministry partners. My own experience has taught me that the commitment of time and energy in sharing this ministry with others has been one of the most rewarding experiences I've had in ministry. It is not necessary that the minister or key leader have a substantial knowledge to make a beginning. All that is needed is a hunger to learn and willingness to do messy ministry.

5. *Making sure the voice of personal testimony is frequently heard will help smooth the path forward.*

We've all lived our lives in a commercialized culture where every product or service is delivered with a carefully groomed sales pitch. In addition, we've taken the bait of advertising only to be disappointed in the end. The culture has taught us caution, and to have a healthy suspicion. We pay more attention when someone we know and respect tells us about a good restaurant, or a movie we should see, or vacation spot to visit.

In the church, every minister has one or more aspects of ministry that have been particularly fulfilling. This is no surprise, and it is true of me. More compelling than my own voice on the subject of preparation for baptism has been what others have shared about their own experience in it. I have listened to parents and sponsors share about how it brought a deeper significance in their understanding of their own baptism, how it enriched their family life, and how it contributed to both parents forming a shared spiritual vision for their children. What others say about what they have experienced will do as much or more to deepen and establish this ministry in a church than a minister's personal advocacy. For this reason, leaders will want to encourage those experiencing this preparation to give personal witness to the experience. This can be done in a newsletter, a thank you note to the session, something spoken during stewardship time, or any opportunity where a group of people are gathered for study or fellowship.

In keeping with the value of such testimony, I asked Becki Williams, a member of the church I now serve, to share her insights and experience of this ministry. Becki is a college chemistry professor who possesses remarkable gifts of listening and hospitality. She is a consummate teacher in the model of Parker Palmer. For more than a dozen years, Becki has partnered with me in leading a team of church members responsible for all ministries that prepare people for baptism, as well as faith formation ministries preparing those already baptized to reaffirm their baptism as they become church members. Though she is not a member of the professional clergy, Becki lives out all she does (including what happens in her chemistry lab) as part of God's call given her at baptism.

A Word of Testimony by Becki Williams

It's with joy and thanksgiving that I reflect upon the twelve years I've participated in baptismal preparation at West Plano Presbyterian Church. Although the primary focus of this volume is given to what comes prior to baptism, I'd like to share how the church's formational ministry with parents who come seeking the baptism of their child has transformed me, the worshipping community, including the children and their parents, and the way we worship and form disciples. I'll offer a few glimpses of the transformation I have witnessed in the hopes of enticing you to embark on this ministry. My belief is that what you experience will surprise you and fill you with wonder.

But first, here is a little background. Before I became a lay leader in this baptism ministry, I served, and continue to serve, as director of our Catechumenate Leadership Team.

This is an intentional ministry of faith exploration, hospitality, and companionship that provides space and time for those discerning God's leading in their lives. In the Bible Belt, where I live, we more often provide this ministry to those who are seeking to reaffirm their baptism in response to an awakened hunger for God. At the center of this ministry, for both seekers and catechists, is discerning together what it means to live *into* and live *out* our baptismal identity. Although certain aspects differ, the formation of adult seekers in the catechumenate process and the preparation for parents seeking baptism for their children both afford opportunities to wonder aloud and often, love questions, nurture the imagination, provide a generous hospitality, treasure the human body, cherish symbols and rituals, enlist and nurture sponsors, and make connections, which results in a reimagination of Christian education as "formation for baptismal living" and a shaping of the Sunday liturgy to welcome all the baptized.

As I engaged with seekers in the catechumenate and preparation for baptism ministries, I came to see my work life as a college chemistry professor as deeply integrated with my baptismal identity. I found that an intensive study of formation with Parker Palmer and his colleagues when he served as a consultant with the community college where I teach, and my experiences as a cooperative learning facilitator were gifts from God that shaped this identity. I embrace gracious hospitality. And the more I am able to offer hospitality and respond to God's call to *form* disciples, the "more like myself I become."

Now to the heart of this reflection: transformation. When we began to reimagine our Christian education experiences as formation for baptismal living, we felt compelled to create our own Vacation Bible School experience. Each year for the last four years, we've designed expeditionary experiences, which we call Little Kids' Camp, with a central theme related to our baptismal identity—water, bread, fire, and, this year, names for God and our names as children of God. The creative design process has given the many adult leaders an opportunity to explore their baptismal identity, reflect on aspects of the preparation for baptism, and engage children and youth in worship and mission in new and novel ways. We gathered around the font each day at the close of camp that first year when we explored water and baptism. After the experience of dipping their thumbs in the font and signing the cross on their foreheads each day, children continued this practice as they moved to receive Communion during worship on Sunday. At the time, many worshippers did not engage in the practice. The children's reverence and commitment to this practice have led some adults to follow their lead.

Though the congregation has not been present in our individual baptism preparation sessions, the process does involve the whole church in acts of blessing and prayer for the child, the families, and the sponsors. The community comes to know, nurture, and care for these children. As these children grow they give witness to their formation—a blessing for adults who worship with them.

Children pray the Ecumenical Lord's Prayer with arms outstretched in the *orans*, they bow before the cross when processing communion elements, they occasionally ask for prayers during the time for intercessory prayer, they hold baskets of bread during the serving of Communion, and they are "at home" with other adults who've accepted responsibility for their spiritual formation at the time of their baptism.

I've been blessed to participate in the weekly closing ritual of the Sunday Studies sessions (our name for Sunday school), where our pre-kindergarten through second-grade children dip their thumbs in a bowl of water, make the sign of the cross on the forehead of another child or adult leader next to them, saying, "[First Name],remember your baptism and be thankful, you belong to God," and then pass the water to the next person to repeat the process until all have been blessed. It's a remarkable experience to be with young children in the presence of God in this way.

My daughter and her husband are members of the church and have participated in the preparation of each of their three young daughters' baptisms. I'm thrilled that this preparation for baptism offers opportunities for them to worship, pray, and celebrate throughout the week in their home with resources to build a liturgical home-life connected with what takes place on Sunday. They light a candle and pray at mealtime using one of the prayers offered in the preparation. There is a bowl of water on the table for splashing and blessing. We celebrate each child's baptismal birthday, often with lavish amounts of water found in puddles, swimming pools, and squirt guns! I lament that our liturgical home-life as parents for our daughter and son were devoid of many of these things. We were ill equipped to be ritual makers without the words, symbols, and rituals that this process provides. However, I praise God for my role as grandmother. I am blessed to hear small voices pray prayers cut a bit too large for them, knowing that they will grow into them in time. It gives me great joy to know these prayers will rest deeply in their memory.

As the author mentioned in the introduction, the formation for baptismal living—be it in structured preparation with families such as this book describes, or in Sunday Studies, Little Kids' Camp, a liturgical home-life, mission, or worship—is lived out, not thought out. This living takes time, reflection, and opportunities for the seeds sown to sprout and grow. The children have led me much of the time with their eager and reverent desire for meaningful participation in the life of the church. Throughout, I've come to know that this process of living into and out of our baptism is a lifelong process of continuing conversion. Daily, I remember my baptism and I am thankful, I belong to God.

Appendix 1:
Sponsors as Spiritual Companions

IN CHAPTER 3 OF this book, I set forth a dozen "matters of special attention underlying this preparation process," of which number 8 was, "Involve others; enlist and nurture sponsors." Sponsors have been an important part of the church's ministry with baptismal candidates since the early church.[1] The communal nature of the Christian faith means that no one comes to God on his or her own; we are brought to Christ by another. James B. Dunning captures this well:

> Before there was a catechumenate, there were sponsors— a sponsoring, welcoming community of people who were convinced that Jesus was Good News for them and that he might be Good News for others. From the year 30 to 180, there was no catechumenal institution as such. ... There were only Christians sharing their lives, sharing both the stories of Jesus and their own faith stories with other people.[2]

Despite the importance of sponsors in the communal transmission of the faith, the common experience of "the church's role as sponsor has been vague and ill-defined," especially so in a

---

1. Tertullian gives a description of Christian initiation and mentions sponsors in connection with children being brought to baptism. See Ferguson, *Baptism in the Early Church*, 2009.

2. Dunning, *New Wine, New Wineskins*, 15, as quoted in Episcopal Church, *Catechumenal Process*, 101.

culture more accustomed than ever to "bowling alone" and being "alone together."³

The baptismal preparation process presented in this book calls for a renewal in the role of sponsors. It envisions them having a place in the ministry of faith formation that both precedes and follows baptism as well as participating in the rite of baptism itself. This ministry is captured in the language of "spiritual companioning."⁴ To help sponsors carry out their role, churches will need to make an investment in training sponsors for this ministry. This appendix offers a short overview and a training outline that can serve as a model for what churches might do to prepare sponsors for their ministry. There are several good resources available that speak of how to recruit sponsors, what to look for, and what their ministry entails.⁵ I will not attempt to duplicate that information here. My interest is offering an accessible way for church leaders to prepare those called to be sponsors for the important role they have in the lives of those preparing for baptism.

Many (perhaps most) sponsors have a sense of inadequacy with respect to such a ministry. In part this is because they think sponsorship requires that they be competent to explain the faith to others. Like most of us, sponsors also are all too aware of their own spiritual failings and feel uncomfortable in any role that suggests they be looked at as examples of what might seem Christian perfection. There is a problem if this is how we understand what being an example entails.

There is no spiritual hierarchy in a sponsor's ministry as a spiritual companion. Instead, sponsorship implies a shared hunger for God, openness to God, and a willingness to be vulnerable in

---

3. These two phrases taken from popular book titles have become metaphors for the decline of face to face community in America. See Putnam, *Bowling Alone*, and Turkle, *Alone Together*.

4. I first encountered this compelling name for sponsors in Cunningham "Patristic Catechesis for Baptism," 18.

5. For help on these questions and others relating to the ministry of sponsors, consult the following: Lewinski, *Guide for Sponsors*; *Welcome to Christ: Sponsors Guide*; Wilde, *Finding and Forming Sponsors and Godparents*; Piro, "Sponsoring Candidates for Affirmation of Baptism."

relationships with fellow seekers. We are all works of God's transformation in progress. At the heart of choosing and recruiting persons is the invitation to ongoing conversion, a call to which sponsors, indeed, the whole church, responds. Being a sponsor means being placed at the leading edge of God's recreating work in personal life and being a witness to what God is doing in those seeking baptism.

Sponsors hear and see the discovery of faith taking place in families being drawn to listen more deeply to God's word and for God's call. In this relationship of companionship, sponsors experience God throughout the preparation for baptism, sharing openly of their own lives of faith. This sharing can be understood as growing in spiritual conversation, which is essential to this process. The preparation sessions are designed to draw participants into conversation of a deeply spiritual nature that touches both heart *and soul*.

> To share with someone our experience of God is to share from the deepest part of who we are. It is a rare and precious gift, in both the giving and the receiving. When someone shares himself or herself with us that intimately, we are on holy ground. Those who walk with another on their journey of faith have these privileged encounters with another's soul. Anyone who has experienced friendship on the level of the soul knows that it is truly a gift from God.[6]

What begins within the preparatory process should naturally flow into other social settings so that the preparation sessions do not become the only occasion for such spiritual sharing. As has been seen, the sessions are intended to spark conversation in the homes between parents, and with older children where possible. But the sessions also envision that conversations will be continued as part of the spiritual companionship of sponsors as they live their call outside the scheduled sessions, whether on Sundays during fellowship time, a phone call during the week, or over a cup of coffee at a local shop. Intentionality in relationships is an important feature of the sponsor relationship.

6. Brown and Orr, "Gift of Spiritual Friendship," 19.

Appendix 2: Enrichment Experience for Sponsors

(2 hours)

Introduction, Welcome, and Prayer

The one leading offers an introduction similar to what follows:

> Writer Ann Lamott has said, "I do not at all understand the mystery of grace—only that it meets us where we are but does not leave us where it found us."[1] The relationships we have as members of Christ's body take particular form in any number of ways as we worship and serve together. But the faith we share moves in us and between us through relationships that connect our lives together. These connections are filled with expressions of caring and sharing that impact what and how we believe as faith grows in us over time. One relationship filled with particular intention is that of sponsor to those preparing for baptism. It is this relationship to which God has called you and for which this training has been set aside.
>
> John's Gospel begins with a succession of compelling vignettes in which those who become Jesus' disciples first encounter the Lord. There is the gentle, enticing question of Jesus, "What are you looking for?" Such a question

---

1. Lamott, *Traveling Mercies*, 143.

asks the hearer to search her or his heart for a clearer grasp of one's own longing. There is Jesus' appealing invitation, "Come and see," which is suggestive of a coming to faith that is gradual and substantially experiential. Finally, there is the simple yet important role that seekers play in one another's lives. There is the sharing, the giving witness, and returning to Jesus with one alongside the other. These elements all play a part in the ministry of sponsorship.

Therefore, hear what the Spirit is saying to the church in this reading from John 1:35–42:

> The next day John again was standing with two of his disciples, and as he watched Jesus walk by, he exclaimed, "Look, here is the Lamb of God!" The two disciples heard him say this, and they followed Jesus. When Jesus turned and saw them following, he said to them, "What are you looking for?" They said to him, "Rabbi" (which translated means Teacher), "where are you staying?" He said to them, "Come and see." They came and saw where he was staying, and they remained with him that day. It was about four o'clock in the afternoon. One of the two who heard John speak and followed him was Andrew, Simon Peter's brother. He first found his brother Simon and said to him, "We have found the Messiah" (which is translated Anointed). He brought Simon to Jesus, who looked at him and said, "You are Simon son of John. You are to be called Cephas" (which is translated Peter).

Leader: At the heart of the sponsor relationship is a willingness to enter into spiritual companionship with another. This time of training together is a beginning appreciation for what we are called to give of ourselves in this ministry. Let us pray:

> God of new birth,
> you seed our lives with grace
> and water them with your Spirit
> that we may bear fruit and serve your saving purpose.
> We thank you for those through whom

we have come to a deeper faith.
And now, we are called to be companions with those whose thirst for you draws them to baptism.
By your grace, fill our weakness with your strength, and our anxiousness with your peace;
through Jesus Christ, our Savior and Lord. **Amen.**

Personal Recollection Alone

Take five minutes to recall a time in your life when you were embarking on some new venture in your life. Can you remember how you felt, what you were thinking, what questions you had at the time? Now see if you can remember if there was anyone present in your life at the time who stands out as particularly helpful. Who was that person? What was it about that person that made him or her so important at the time? Was there something he or she did, or said? Was there some special quality that person displayed that benefitted you? Now, a final question: Has there ever been such a helpful person in your life of faith? What difference did that make?

Shared Reflection in Pairs

Breaking into pairs, spend some time sharing the experience which you have recollected as well as the insights you have discovered concerning why this relationship had such meaning for you. In addition, take a few moments to comment on whether you had such a person play a role in your life of faith.

Together as a Group

What has been recalled individually and shared in pairs tells a truth about the significance of relationships to times of ending and beginning in our lives. Preparing for baptism involves cultivating a readiness for the newness of fresh commitment and responsibilities we did not have before. To walk this path with another is a gift and a blessing. Sponsors offer a presence that embodies special qualities that make that companion relationship meaningful.

Leaders will want to hear from the pairs about their sharing, perhaps asking each member of the dyad to offer what he or she heard from the other. Many of the qualities that will be named in this sharing are important to the sponsor relationship. Indeed, the sharing exercise just completed will have made this obvious and it will have given each person practice in the art of listening and attending.

Key Elements of a Sponsor's Ministry

In closing this training session, the following ministry values form a helpful summary. These can be shared by the leader with brief comments taken from the group.

Active Listening

Listening lies at the heart of any significant relationship. Sponsors are called to listen in ways that are discerning. "Discernment requires listening with openness and freedom for God's desire for us, rather than a choice we make. . . . Its focus is on God and God's invitation."[2] Those with whom sponsors are in relation are processing new understanding, new experiences, and new responsibilities that may need time and help to sort out. The listening of the sponsor for how the Spirit may be leading is a gift of this companionship relationship. It not necessary for a sponsor to have all the answers to every question posed. It is best not to give advice but to share in ways that help the person remain open to the Spirit's leading. In this regard, the sponsor trusts God to work through her or him. Listening in this manner is a form of paying attention that imparts a feeling of being accompanied.

---

2. Steffen, *Discerning Disciples*, 8.

Extending Hospitality

Hospitality is one expression of unconditional love. For this reason, it appears again and again as an important virtue in biblical faith. Henri Nouwen says that hospitality is "the creation of a free space where the stranger can enter and become a friend instead of an enemy. Hospitality is not to change people, but to offer them space where change can take place."[3] Fundamental to all hospitality is serving the needs of others before ourselves.

Bearing Witness

By virtue of the Christ in us, we each can bear witness to what God is doing in our lives despite our awareness of being works in progress. We are not called to exhibit perfection; rather, we are called to bear truthful witness to the ways the Spirit is at work in us. Often, the Spirit's working involves struggle, failure, renewal, and challenge. So authentic witness involves sharing how God has picked us up when we have fallen and given us the strength to start anew. Putting our personal faith stories to speech (which is what bearing witness entails) is an important practice that deepens our faith even as it witnesses to it. Tom Long has written, "We talk our way *toward* belief, talk our way from tentative belief through doubt to firmer belief, toward believing more fully, more clearly, more deeply. Putting things into words is one of the ways we acquire knowledge, passion, and conviction."[4] However strong or weak we may feel our faith to be, we are able to share the confidence we find in the fact that "there is more mercy in God than sin in us."[5]

---

3 Nouwen, *Reaching Out*, 51.

4. Long, *Testimony*, 6.

5. Coffin, *Credo*, 85.

Appendix 2: Enrichment Experience for Sponsors

Building Bridges

Sponsors are generous in their ministry, looking for ways to connect the ones with whom they are related to other people in the church. In fact, their role is to build relational bridges that facilitate broader and deeper connections in the community. This requires a thoughtfulness that is alert to opportunities where introductions can be made, invitations given, conversations expanded, and groups opened up to include new life. Sponsors are proactive in this regard, not waiting for things to happen on their own.

Offering Guidance

Learning the ways the baptizing community lives out its life can be confusing. Those new to the church will have many questions and will need to know it is safe to ask any of them. It is not necessary that sponsors have all the answers from their own pool of personal knowledge or experience. Whenever needed, sponsors will have the necessary connections to go to the right person for the information. In this way, the guidance given by sponsors involves learning how to navigate within the faith community to the resources needed.

Bibliography

Archbishop's Council. *Common Worship: Services and Prayers for the Church of England*. London: Church House Publishing, 2000.
Atwood, Margaret. *The Penelopiad: The Myth of Penelope and Odysseus*. New York:L Canongate, 2005.
Baker, J. Robert, Evelyn Kaehler, and Peter Mazar, eds. *A Lent Sourcebook: The Forty Days*. Book 2. Chicago: Liturgy Training Publications, 1990.
Bass, Diana Butler. *Christianity After Religion: The End of Church and the Birth of a New Spiritual Awakening*. New York: HarperOne, 2012.
Batchelder, David. "Sacramental Liturgy and Its Continuing Incarnation in Mission." *Call to Worship* 44:4 (2011) 1–9.
Berry, Wendell. "How to Be a Poet." In *Given: New Poems*, 18–19. Berkeley, CA: Counterpoint, 2005.
Brown, Kathleen H., and David M. Orr. "The Gift of Spiritual Friendship." *Ministry and Liturgy* 33:7 (September 2006) 19.
Budde, Michael L. *The (Magic) Kingdom of God: Christianity and Global Cultural Industries*. Boulder, CO: Westview, 1997.
Byars, Ronald. "Indiscriminate Baptism and Baptismal Integrity." *Reformed Liturgy and Music* 31 (1997) 36–40.
Calvin, John. "Excerpt from 'A Short Treatise on the Lord's Supper.'" In *John Calvin: Writings on Pastoral Piety*, translated and edited by Elsie Anne McKee, 104–11. New York: Paulist, 2001.
———. *Institutes of the Christian Religion*. Translated by Henry Beveridge. Vol. 2. Grand Rapids: Eerdmans, 1974.
———. "Short Treatise on the Supper of Our Lord Jesus Christ." In *John Calvin: Selections from His Writings*, edited by Emelie Griffin, translated by Elsie Anne McKee, 57–65. San Francisco: HarperSanFrancisco, 2006.
Church of Scotland, Office for Worship and Doctrine. *A Welcome to a Child: Four Orders for Thanksgivings and Blessings*. Edinburgh: Saint Andrews Press, 2006.
Coffin, William Sloane, Jr. *Credo*. Louisville: Westminster John Knox, 2004.
———. *Letters to a Young Doubter*. Louisville: Westminster John Knox, 2005.

BIBLIOGRAPHY

Coleman, Lyman. *Encyclopedia of Serendipity*. Littleton, CO: Serendipity House, 1976.

Cunningham, Agnes. "Patristic Catechesis for Baptism: A Pedagogy for Christian Living." In *Before and After Baptism: The Work of Teachers and Catechists*, edited by James A. Wilde, 15-25. Chicago: Liturgy Training, 1988.

Duggan, Robert D., ed. *Conversion and the Catechumenate*. New York: Paulist, 1984.

Dunning, James B. *New Wine, New Wineskins: Pastoral Implications of the Rite of Christian Initiation of Adults*. New York: Sadlier, 1981.

Espada, Martin. "The Republic of Poetry: Hampshire College Commencement Address." Commencement address given at Hampshire College, Amherst, MA, May 19, 2007. http://sarahbrowning.blogspot.com/2007/05/republic-of-poetry-martn-espadas.html.

Episcopal Church, Office of Evangelism Ministries. *The Catechumenal Process: Adult Initiation & Formation for Christian Life and Ministry*. New York: Church Hymnal Corporation, 1990.

Episcopal Church, Standing Liturgical Commission. *Book of Occasional Services, 1994*. New York: Church Publishing, 1995.

———. *Book of Occasional Services, 2003*. New York: Church Publishing, 2003.

Evangelical Lutheran Church in America (ELCA). *Evangelical Lutheran Worship*. Leader's Desk Edition. Minneapolis: Augsburg Fortress, 2006.

———. *The Use of the Means of Grace: A Statement on the Practice of Word and Sacrament*. Minneapolis: Augsburg Fortress, 1997.

Ferguson, Everett. *Baptism in the Early Church: History, Theology, and Liturgy in the First Five Centuries*. Grand Rapids: Eerdmans, 2009.

General Directory for Catechesis. Bangalore: Theological Publications in India, 2011.

Harmless, William. *Augustine and the Catechumenate*. Collegeville: Liturgical, 1995.

Hovda, Robert. *The Amen Corner*. Collegeville: Liturgical, 1994.

Hunsinger, George. *The Eucharist and Ecumenism: Let Us Keep the Feast*. Cambridge: Cambridge University Press, 2008.

Jespersen, Richard A. *I Am Baptized*. Lima, OH: CSS, 2000.

Kavanagh, Aiden. *Elements of Rite: A Handbook of Liturgical Style*. New York: Pueblo, 1982.

———. *The Shape of Baptism: The Rite of Christian Initiation*. New York: Pueblo, 1978.

Keifer, Ralph A., William J. Freburger and Joseph L. Caulfield, eds. *The Liturgy of the Hours: Morning Prayer, Evening Prayer, Night Prayer*. Translated by the International Committee on English in the Liturgy. Collegeville, MN: Liturgical, 1976.

Kreider, Alan. *The Change of Conversion and the Origin of Christendom*. Harrisburg, PA: Trinity, 1999.

BIBLIOGRAPHY

Lamott, Anne. *Traveling Mercies: Some Thoughts on Faith.* New York: Anchor, 1999.

Larkin, Phillip. "Water". http://allpoetry.com/poem/8495701-Water-by-Philip_Larkin.

L'Engle, Madeleine. *Walking on Water: Reflections on Faith and Art.* Wheaton, IL: Harold Shaw, 1980.

Lewinski, Ron. *Guide for Sponsors.* Chicago: Liturgy Training Publications, 2008.

Long, Thomas G. *Testimony: Talking Ourselves into Being Christian.* San Francisco: Jossey-Bass, 2004.

Miller, Vincent J. *Consuming Religion: Christian Faith and Practice in a Consumer Culture.* New York: Continuum, 2009.

Mitchell, Nathan. "A Trinity of Themes." *Worship* 86:1 (January 2012) 74.

Monastero di Bose. "Friend, guest or pilgrim." http://www.monasterodibose.it/en/hospitality.

Murphy, Debra Dean. *Teaching That Transforms: Worship as the Heart of Christian Education.* Grand Rapids: Brazos, 2004.

Nelson, C. Ellis. *Where Faith Begins.* Richmond: John Knox, 1967.

Nouwen, Henri. *Reaching Out: The Three Movements of the Spiritual Life.* Garden City, NY: Doubleday, 1975.

Piro, Beverly. "Sponsoring Candidates for Affirmation of Baptism." In *What Do You Seek?: Welcoming the Adult Inquirer: A Guide to Ministry with New Members,* edited by Dennis Bushkofsky, 43–50. Minneapolis: Augsburg Fortress, 2000.

Presbyterian Church (USA). *Book of Common Worship.* Louisville: Westminster/John Knox, 1993.

———. *Book of Order.* Constitution of the Presbyterian Church (U.S.A.) Part II. 2015–2017. Louisville: Office of the General Assembly, 2015.

———. *Invitation to Christ: A Guide to Sacramental Practices.* Louisville: Presbyterian Church (USA), 2006.

Presbyterian Church (USA), General Assembly Council. *Discerning the Spirit, Envisioning Our Future: A Report to the Church.* Presented at the Convocation of the Presbyterian Church (USA), Chicago, October 30–November 1, 1992. Louisville: General Assembly Council, 1992.

Presbyterian Church (USA) and Cumberland Presbyterian Church. *Daily Prayer: The Worship of God.* Supplemental Liturgical Resource 5. Philadelphia: Westminster, 1987.

Putnam, Robert D. *Bowling Alone: The Collapse and Revival of American Community.* New York: Simon & Schuster, 2000.

Rilke, Rainer Maria. *Letters to a Young Poet.* Translated by Stephen Mitchell. New York: Random House, 1984.

Robinson, Marilynne. *Gilead.* New York: Picador, 2004.

Schmemann, Alexander. *Of Water and the Spirit: A Liturgical Study of Baptism.* Crestwood, NY: St. Vladamir's Seminary Press, 1986.

Searle, Mark. "Infant Baptism Reconsidered." In *Alternative Futures for Worship*, vol. 2, *Baptism and Confirmation*, edited by Mark Searle, 15–54. Collegeville, MN: Liturgical, 1987.

———. *Vision: The Scholarly Contributions of Mark Searle to Liturgical Renewal*. Edited by Anne Y. Koester and Barbara Searle. Collegeville, MN: Liturgical, 2004.

Smith, James K. A. *Desiring the Kingdom: Worship, Worldview, and Cultural Formation*. Cultural Liturgies 1. Grand Rapids: Baker Academic, 2009.

Steffen, Donna. *Discerning Disciples: Listening for God's Voice in Christian Initiation*. 2nd ed. Chicago: Liturgy Training Publications, 2004.

Tarasar, Constance. "Taste and See: Orthodox Children at Worship." In *The Sacred Play of Children*, edited by Diane Apostolos-Cappadona, 43–54. New York: Seabury, 1983.

Tertullian. "On Baptism." Translated by Rev. S. Thelwall. In *The Ante-Nicene Fathers*, edited by Alexander Roberts and James Donaldson, 3:669–79. Grand Rapids: Eerdmans, 1978.

———. "Resurrection of the Flesh." Translated by Dr. Holmes. In *The Ante-Nicene Fathers*, edited by Alexander Roberts and James Donaldson, 3:545–95. Grand Rapids: Eerdmans, 1978.

Turkle, Sherry. *Alone Together: Why We Expect More from Technology and Less from Each Other*. New York: Basic Books, 2011.

Warren, Michael. *Faith, Culture, and the Worshiping Community*. New York: Paulist, 1989.

Weil, Louis. "Children and Worship." In *The Sacred Play of Children*, edited by Diane Apostolos-Cappadona, 55–59. New York: Seabury, 1983.

Welcome to Christ: Sponsors Guide. Minneapolis: Augsburg Fortress, 2002.

Wilde, James A., ed. *Finding and Forming Sponsors and Godparents*. Chicago: Liturgy Training Publications, 1988.

Williams, Rowan. *Where God Happens: Discovering Christ in One Another*. Boston: New Seeds, 2007.

Wood, Douglas. *Old Turtle and the Broken Truth*. New York: Scholastic, 2003.

Yarnold, Edward. *The Awe-Inspiring Rites of Initiation: The Origins of the R.C.I.A.* 2nd ed. Collegeville, MN: Liturgical, 1994.

www.ingramcontent.com/pod-product-compliance
Lightning Source LLC
Chambersburg PA
CBHW071507150426
43191CB00009B/1443